MW00629388

Things Don't Just Happen

Robby Stephens

A Good Word
A Ministry of Encouragement

A Ministry of A Good Word, Inc.

© Copyright 2009, Robby Stephens

All Rights Reserved.

No part of this book may be reproduced, stored in a
retrieval system, or transmitted by any means,
electronic, mechanical, photocopying, recording,
or otherwise, without written permission
from the author.

ISBN: 978-0-578-01503-3

Scripture quotations marked (NIV) are taken from the HOLY BIBLE, NEW
INTERNATIONAL VERSION®. NIV®. Copyright© 1973, 1978, 1984 by
International Bible Society. Used by permission of Zondervan. All rights reserved.
The Message by Eugene H. Peterson, copyright (c) 1993, 1994, 1995, 1996, 2000, 2001,
2002. Used by permission of NavPress Publishing Group. All rights reserved.
Scripture quotations marked NLT are taken from the Holy Bible, New Living
Translation, copyright 1996, 2004. Used by permission of Tyndale House Publishers,
Inc., Wheaton, Illinois 60189. All rights reserved.
Scripture taken from the New King James Version. Copyright © 1982 by Thomas
Nelson, Inc. Used by permission. All rights reserved.
"Revised Standard Version of the Bible, copyright 1952 [2nd edition, 1971] by the
Division of Christian Education of the National Council of the Churches of Christ in
the United States of America. Used by permission. All rights reserved."
Good News Translation - Second Edition
Copyright (c) 1992 by American Bible Society. Used by permission
Scripture quotations are taken from the Holman Christian Standard Bible®, Copyright
© 1999, 2000, 2002, 2003 by Holman Bible Publishers. Used by permission.

Dedicated to

Julie Stephens

Julie is my loving wife, editor, and encourager. She is a living example of the truth of the Word:

"Wives, in the same way be submissive to your husbands so that, if any of them do not believe the word, they may be won over without words by the behavior of their wives, when they see the purity and reverence of your lives." 1 Peter 3:1-2

Jana,
You are in my prayers!
There _is_ a purpose
and plan for your
life! [signature]
(James 4:8)

Introduction

It is my sincere hope that reading this book will bring you closer to God, and you will come to understand that the Bible still applies to every aspect of our lives today. In Bible times, people experienced the same trials, illnesses, disappointments, and doubt that you and I experience today. Many people say it is "the little things in life that mean the most." I have found that God uses the little things in life to teach me lessons for everyday living, and I want to share these stories with you so your faith will increase and so that you, too, will start noticing the little things around you that are not just coincidences. Things don't just happen.

I am a 50-year-old husband and father of two. I have been married 29 years to a wonderful wife and mother, Julie. She teaches 8th grade social studies at Mabry Middle School and loves working with young people. My son, Josh, is a graduate of Georgia Southern University and works as a State Farm Insurance representative in Woodstock, Georgia. My daughter, Jenna, will complete her degree in Communications at Kennesaw State University in 2009. I graduated from Georgia Southern University in 1980 with a BBA Degree in Marketing, and I work as a sales manager for an Atlanta, Georgia Oil Company.

I am currently enrolled in Luther Rice Seminary working toward completion of a Master of Arts in Ministry degree. I am involved in several student ministries, one of which I lead as Chairman, of the college ministry with the Kennesaw State University Wesley Foundation. I teach weekly Sunday school lessons. I also have a web ministry called "A Good Word" which seeks to provide encouragement to many readers across the world.

Contents

Foreword

Robby has been a dear friend and accountability partner for years. He has been a wonderful encouragement and blessing in my life. I have been greatly inspired by his writings. This book is a compilation of lessons and "words of encouragement" written to encourage and inspire young and old alike. The Bible says in 3 John 4, "There is no greater joy than to hear of my children walking in truth." Robby has been a witness to many people "walking in truth" as a result of his life, encouragement and teaching. As a college pastor, friend, and partner in ministry, it has been a joy to see how Robby has encouraged so many people through his writings.

I have been trying to get Robby to publish these writings for years. It's about time! You will be blessed, encouraged, challenged and inspired!

Johnny Condrey
Minister, SCORE International, Inc.
www.gapyearinternational.com
Woodstock, GA

Things Don't Just Happen

I enjoyed writing this first lesson. It actually turned into my Sunday school lesson for my class at church one Sunday. I wanted to start my book off with this lesson for a reason: I truly believe the title. After you read several of my real life true stories, you will soon discover how there must be a Higher authority lining up these events. The inspiration for this lesson came from several "life lessons" and from an e-mail written by a college student friend of mine. For several years, I taught a Sunday school class every Sunday for the College and Young Adults at my church. I especially love teaching this age because of the wonderful questions that I receive. Young adults are entering a phase of life when they begin to seek more in depth answers. It is at this juncture when one may choose the teachings of "the world in which we live" or what the Word of God says.

College professors teach mainly from the books of man, which advocate that all of life's answers are found through science and math. This leads directly into the e-mail that I received. The stude'nt who wrote this e-mail is an outstanding student in one of the finest technology schools in the country. I had just finished a Sunday school lesson about how God works through what seems to be coincidences to us.

The e-mail reads, "—I would just like to say that one concept that really hit me this week during Sunday school was the idea that coincidences are not always just probability. I know that it must seem obvious to you when they happen, but I had always assumed that mathematics/physics dictates everything." This e-mailed blessed me. This is what "the world in which we live" teaches.

I was studying the Book of Ruth this week, and I came across something in chapter two that caught my attention. It is in the story of Ruth. Ruth loses her husband tragically, is caught in the middle of a famine, and has to move to a foreign land. It seems that she's pretty down on her luck. No blessings going on here, right? Scientifically, a famine, and statistically, an unmarried widowed female, Ruth is spiraling down to a point that she just won't make it. She seems doomed to just happen to be crushed by life itself. Her only hope at the time is in Naomi, her mother in law.

But read Ruth 2:1-3. The King James Version gives these verses a significant message: "And Naomi had a kinsman of her husband's, a mighty man of wealth, of the family of Elimelech; and his name was Boaz. And Ruth the Moabites said unto Naomi, 'Let me now go to the field, and glean ears of corn after him whose sight I shall find grace. And she said unto her, Go, my daughter. And she went, and came, and gleaned in the field after the reapers: and her hap was to light on a part of the field belonging unto Boaz, who was of the kindred of Elimelech."

Did you catch it? You see, Ruth is going into a field to gather grains of corn left by the reapers. She and Naomi need these grains just to survive. But God has bigger plans. In verse three, which is the last sentence above, the Bible says that Ruth "hap" (happened) to go into a field that was owned by Boaz, a very wealthy man of God. Hmmm! Just happened to go to the field of Boaz??

You may say, "Robby, you have my attention. Is there any other "happens" in this story?" I'm glad that you asked! Yes, there is. Boaz goes over to his men and asks who that woman is in his field. He finds out her name and where she is from. Then Boaz goes over to greet Ruth. He tells Ruth that she is welcomed in his field, and for her to follow his reapers so that she may get more corn as it is left behind. Then the Bible says in Ruth 2:10, "She dropped to her knees, then bowed her face to the ground. 'How does this happen that you should pick me out and treat me so kindly-me a foreigner.'" (The Message) There is that "happened" word again.

The Word of encouragement today is that things don't just happen for the believers who walk in the ways of the Lord. Some of these "happens" seem to be bad at the time. I don't have the answers to why things may have happened in your life that were full of hurt. I can tell you that now that I look back on my life, I'm beginning to see the answers to questions like that. I see why certain things happened in my life to get me where I am now in my walk with Christ Jesus. Ruth certainly couldn't see any positives in the tragedies that she went through at the time. Are you in a trial that you can't understand right now?

Stay full of faith! Ask God for His direction. Give it over to God to work out in His perfect way. The Bible says in Psalms 27: 14: "Wait for the Lord; be strong, and let your heart take courage, wait for the Lord!"

The story of Ruth ends in a wonderful "happenstance". Boaz marries Ruth, and Ruth becomes the owner of the field where she was once picking up the grains left behind just to survive. With one stroke of God's favor, leading Ruth to "hap" in the field owned by Boaz, Ruth became blessed way beyond her imagination. While married to Boaz, Ruth gave birth to a child, a son named Obed. Obed was the father of Jesse. Jesse was the father of King David. (Read Matthew chapter 1, the genealogy of Jesus.) Ruth was a grandmother of our Lord Jesus! Could that have just happened? Ask your statistics professor to run the probability of that to happen.

God happens to love you very much. Walk in His ways and look for the things that happen in your life. God will lead you to the field that is "hap" for your life. Things don't just happen! You didn't just happen to get a copy of this book...keep reading. The Message is for you!

Divine Deliberate Delays

The above picture is an accurate portrayal of our lives in this world. We are generally coming out of a storm, going into a storm, or in the middle of a storm. Which direction would you guess that this boat is headed? If your current situation is like this boat, be very glad for the peaceful waters that you are in at this time. If your waters are currently calm, you may even think that you don't need to read this lesson right now; but the waves may get rough very soon.

I like smooth waters. If you know me at all, you'll know that real storms actually scare me. (Read my lesson called *A Nail As An Anchor* to see where this fear started.) I don't like the stormy weather times of life either. If my life were the boat above, I would be paddling just as hard as I could toward the direction of the open sky. But unfortunately storms seem to always catch up to us. If your life seems to be in a storm just now, I've got A Good Word for you!

Sometimes we place ourselves in storms by the choices that we make. There are consequences for our chosen actions. Once in the storm, we'll still have choices to make to get through it. We can ride it out on our own, and hopefully we won't get dumped out to sink or swim. Or, we can seek the One who can say, "Quiet! Be still!" Then the wind died down and it was completely calm" (Mark 4:39 NIV).

You may be thinking right now, "Robby, I'm in a terrible storm, and I didn't do anything to bring it about. All I know is that I want out. I've been asking in my prayers for delivery from this storm, but I see no good results, only delays. My faith may be what is actually sinking in this storm." If this is where you are, I say hold on; help is on the way. Did you know that you might have been deliberately placed in this storm by Divine Providence? Perhaps there is a Divine Deliberate Delay for your rescue?

In the Book of Matthew, chapter 14 there is a story about the disciples of Jesus being Divinely placed into a storm. The Bible says, "Immediately Jesus made the disciples get into the boat and go ahead of him to the other side ..." (Matthew 14:22). This passage caught my attention this week. Why would Jesus MAKE the disciples get into the boat, which seemingly looked like they were going out alone without Him? Let's keep reading: "his disciples went down to the lake, where they got into a boat and set off across the lake for Capernaum. By now it was dark, and Jesus had not yet joined them. A strong wind was blowing and the waters grew rough" (John 6:16-18). Now why would Jesus send His loved ones out seemingly alone into a storm? Why might you be out in a storm and you feel all alone?

The Bible goes on to say, "When they had rowed three or three and a half miles, ..." (I'm sure that they were trying to row themselves out of that storm, like I said would do in the picture above) "they saw Jesus approaching the boat, walking on the water; and they were terrified. But he said to them, "It is I; don't be afraid"" (John 6:19-20). This story ends with a very interesting note– "Then they were willing to take him into the boat, and immediately the boat reached the shore where they were heading" (v. 21). Here these guys are struggling to row through the storm, and as soon as Jesus climbs into the boat, the boat reaches the shore. Again I ask, what was the purpose of placing them into a deliberate storm? The answer can be found in Matthew 14:33: "Then those who were in the boat worshiped him, saying, 'Truly you are the Son of God.'"

This was a Divine Deliberate storm, but why the delay for rescue? Our rescues are delayed often so we have the opportunity to truly see the Lord's hand in our rescue. The first Bible story that I mentioned above, from Mark 4:39, is about a different storm when Jesus was actually traveling in the boat with the disciples. Perhaps in that story I would have been more like the disciple Thomas, and tried to reason that perhaps just as Jesus said, "Quiet! Be still!" the wind "coincidentally" stopped at the same moment. In my personal testimony, on the day of April 4, 1997, my Divine Deliberate Delay ended, and I was rescued to see and understand Who should be in charge of my life. There was no "coincidence" in my delivery.

You can find another Divine Deliberate Delay in the Book of John, chapter 11. This is a story about a man named Lazarus. Jesus loved Lazarus and his sisters, Mary and Martha. Lazarus became very sick and Mary sent word to Jesus to come immediately: "So the sister sent word to Jesus, 'Lord, the one you love is sick.' When he heard this, Jesus said, 'This sickness will not end in death. No, it is for God's glory so that God's Son may be glorified through it.' Jesus loved Martha and her sister and Lazarus" (John 11:3-5). You may think, "Robby, I suppose Jesus went right away to heal His beloved Lazarus? He wouldn't deliberately allow any of His loved ones to have to face any bad storms would He? He certainly wouldn't have any Divine Delay here would He? The Bible says next, "Yet when he heard that Lazarus was sick, he stayed where he was two more days" (v. 6). Lazarus died!

The Bible says, "On his arrival, Jesus found that Lazarus had already been in the tomb for four days"(v. 17). I would certainly call this a delay. Martha meets Jesus at His arrival and says, "Lord, ... if you had been here, my brother would not have died" (v.21). Verse 16 of this story says that the disciple Thomas was with Jesus. I believe again that I may have been like Thomas if Jesus would have arrived before the death of Lazarus, and Jesus healed Lazarus of his sickness. Just maybe I would have thought, "I know that Lazarus was healed, but maybe it was time for him to get better?"

No, the Delay was Divine. Jesus says to Martha, "I am the resurrection and the life. He who believes in me will live, even though he dies; and whoever lives and believes in me will never die" (v.25-26). Jesus raised a man from the dead who had been in the tomb for four days. The Bible says that many placed their faith in Jesus that day. There was no "coincidence" in that Divine Deliberate Delay.

Now you may think, "Robby, those are very encouraging stories, but I just don't think that Jesus can see me in my storm. I think that my storm is just too strong for Him to see to get to me. The waves are too big for even Him to walk on. I wish I knew where He was now?" I can tell you! The Bible tells us in Hebrews 7:25 that Jesus is praying (interceding) for us: "Therefore he is able to save completely those who come to God through him, because he always lives to intercede for them." I love it each time the Bible says "always." He is able to save you completely from your storm. He can see you now in your storm, no matter how severe it is, and He is interceding for you. You ask how do I know?

Back to the story about sending the disciples into the storm… This same story is told in the Gospels of Matthew, Mark, and John. In the Gospel of Mark the Bible says, "After leaving them, he went up on a mountainside to pray. (Now Jesus is praying.) When the evening came, the boat was in the middle of the lake, and he was alone on land. (Watch this now.) He saw the disciples straining at the oars, because the wind was against them" (Mark 6:46-48). He sees us through the storm! He sees you straining at the oars as you seek your way out of the storm. Isn't it interesting that the Bible would tell us that the boat was in the "middle" of the lake, and He saw the disciples straining against the wind? (This is a HUGE lake, Sea of Galilee.)

I say hang in there! Keep steady in the Divine direction that you are headed. Don't let the strong winds of doubt allow you to drift off course. Start looking for Jesus to show up even though there has been what seems a delay. When you first get a glimpse of His presence, be prepared to be full of faith to jump out of your boat and walk with Him in your storm. Be willing to take Him into your boat (your life) and you will immediately reach the shore where you were Divinely headed. Just as I did in 1997, you too will then say, "Truly you are the Son of God."

Home Field Advantage

The new fall football season is upon us. I'm actually writing this lesson on the first day of fall 2005. It's been hot and dry here in the Atlanta area, so it hasn't really felt like a fall day yet. The evenings are getting nice, however.

But fall means football season is upon us. Have you been watching your favorite team? Perhaps you have attended a game. If you follow sports at all, you understand the significance of a home game. All of your own fans fill the stands and cheer for the home team. I played on many sports teams during high school, and I fully appreciate the value of playing a home game. There was a wonderful warm feeling of encouragement when the home fans would cheer for the efforts of the players. As a player, we especially needed that encouragement after playing an away game.

The away games were played on the opponent's turf. The opponent's fans were hostile. We played against the enemy, on the enemy's home field. It was always nice to come home.

Do you realize that your life is very much like this today? Your away games are the day-to-day living in the world in which you live. Your away games are played out on the enemy's home field. Jesus tells us in the Book of John that Satan is the ruler of this world. In John 14, Jesus is speaking of His death and His sending of the Holy Spirit. He says in verse 30, "I cannot talk with you much longer, because the ruler of this world is coming. He has no power over me" (Good News Translation).

The Apostle Paul is speaking about our away game battle with Satan and his demons in the Book of Ephesians 6:12: "For we are not fighting against human beings but against the wicked spiritual forces in the heavenly world, the rulers, authorities, and cosmic power of this dark age." Paul goes on to tell us in the following four verses about the protective equipment that we had better put on to help us in our away game battle, and the list includes a helmet! "So put on God's armor now! Then when the evil day comes, you will be able to resist the enemy's attacks; and after fighting to the end, you will still hold your ground" (v. 6:13). Kind of sounds like a football coach's motivation speech to me. "So stand ready, with truth as a belt tight around your waist, with righteousness as your breastplate, and your shoes the readiness to announce the Good News of peace. At all times carry faith as a shield; for with it you will be able to put out all the burning arrows shot by the Evil One. And accept salvation as a helmet, and the word of God as the sword which the spirit gives you" (v. 6:14-17).

So with our equipment on, we are able to take on our opponent in the away games. You have the "Good News of peace" within you as a believer in Jesus Christ as your savior. Therefore, "the one who is in you is greater than the one who is in the world" (1 John 4: 4). You have the ability now to take on the hostile crowd and the enemy in the away game battle and win! Winning is always nice on an away game, but it's always nice to come back home to the home fans and supporters. The away games are tough, and you do get banged up and bruised.

You may be thinking, "Well Robby, I understand now about the away games, but where are our home games? Where do we go to feel the support of the home crowd?" The answer is your local church. You just may not understand how important it is for you to go and receive the home field advantage at least one day each week. You play away games all week long; you need to have a home game at least one day per week to get refreshed, and most importantly, to get renewed. Without this one day of refreshment, you can become worn down in your daily battles. As you become worn down, this means that your defense has been on the field too long. You may start getting weak and allowing the enemy to penetrate into your territory. At this point you will begin to give in and begin to be "conformed," or a part of, this world.

Paul tells us in Romans 12: 2: "And do not be conformed to this world, but be transformed by the renewing of your mind, that you may prove what is that good and acceptable and perfect will of God" (New King James Version). In church and Sunday school you hear the Word of God, and your mind is renewed. The home team and the home team crowd also join you. You receive the home game encouragement and fellowship. (You can't receive this by watching a sermon on the television.) The Book of Hebrews tells us what to do in our home games. In chapter 10: 24-25, the Bible says, "And let us consider how we may spur one another on toward love and good deeds. Let us not give up meeting together, as some are in the habit of doing, but let us encourage one another..." The Bible tells us here to "not give up meeting together." Therefore, it's there for a reason! It is important to receive that home field advantage.

I would like to encourage you today to make it a point to go to church each week. You may be away from home at college. You may be out of school in one of your first jobs. You may be one that has just not attended church in a while, or possibly ever. In all of these cases, it is important for you to find a church that teaches the Bible. I can't think of any team that would prefer to play all of their games at an away, hostile field. Go receive the home field advantage.

Finding Sharks Teeth

The air is warming, school is winding down, and summer must be near. This gets me excited about looking forward to one of my favorite things to do—go to the beach. I love the beach and everything about the coast. The one thing that I'm not crazy about is just lying around in one spot working on a tan. I will, however, sit and read a good book.

My favorite activity, though, is something that I picked up just a few years ago. I can spend hours doing it, and I do each year. What do you see in the picture above? Look closely. Can you see it? There it is right in front of you! Can you see it?

The picture above is about what the sand looks like in many spots along the beach in Fernandina Beach, Florida. For years we would go to Fernandina Beach and I would walk across a place in the sand like this and never see it. But now I am a trained expert at finding sharks' teeth in the sand. These are very small, and the color of the sand as well. They blend in with the sand so well that if you don't train yourself to see them you will never find one. In other words, you have to look for them to see them. They are all over the sand. I mean to tell you that there are hundreds of them. Each year I collect several on each trip. (I don't understand why so many sharks lose their teeth at Fernandina Beach?)

I can't tell you the number of times that other people will come up to me and ask me, "What are you looking for?" And I'll tell them, "Sharks' teeth." They will give me a very strange "I don't believe you" look, and then I will show them one in my hand. They will immediately start looking down at the sand trying to find one. The thing that I've observed over the years, is that when they start looking, they only look for about a minute and then they give up and walk away, never seeing what was right in front of them.

Did you know that seeing God's blessings in your life could be just like this? You see, just as I have trained my eyes to see sharks' teeth in the sand, I have trained myself to see God's blessings that He bestows upon me each and every day. Now I'm not just talking about the obvious blessings like my health, my family's health, my job, my home, etc. (Those are GREAT and most appreciated.) I'm talking about the hidden blessings that God has for each and every one of us (His favor) if we look for them. The thing is, you have to train yourself to see them as well.

The Bible says in Psalms 5:12, "For surely, O Lord, you bless the righteous: you surround them with your favor as with a shield" (NIV). The scripture says the Lord blesses the righteous. What does righteous mean? The late, great, first coach of the Georgia Southern Eagles football team, Erk Russell, was a talented motivational speaker. He often told his team this simple saying, "Do right."

First you must "do right" in the eyes of the Lord. You do this by obeying His Word. What I want to "coach" you on today is how to see God's favor (blessings) surrounding you "as with a shield." This takes a joint effort on your part as well.

You may be thinking, "Now I would love to believe that the Lord can give me a shield of His favor. But I wonder what it would be like, and how do I find it?" Just like training your eyes to see the sharks' teeth, you must train yourself to see the blessings. This takes practice as well, especially if you've been training yourself to look at all the negatives in life. Proverbs 15:15 says, "All the days of the oppressed are wretched, but the cheerful heart has a continual feast."

Webster defines "oppressed" as "to burden spiritually or mentally: weigh heavily upon." Do you feel oppressed often? Do you tend to look at the negative things that are happening in your life? Are you spiritually and mentally loaded down with weight? If this is you, then seeing any blessings in your life may look like that glob of sand in the picture above. You just can't see the shark's tooth. I have A Good Word for you!

"The cheerful heart has a continual feast." A continual feast…I like that thought. A cheerful heart has continual blessings and most importantly a continued spirit of walking with the Lord. "But Robby," you may ask, "how do I get back that cheerful heart when at times I feel so spiritually burdened?" First, I will tell you how you won't get the cheerful heart back. (Why do I start off with how you won't get it back?) I tell you because the first thing that you want to do will be to get by yourself (all alone). How do I know this? This is biblical.

What character in the Bible do we think of when we think of terrible trials and deep spiritual and mental depression? (Job.) In the Book of Job, Job is replying to his "friends" that are trying to help him. He just tells them, "Leave me alone …" Then, "Why then have you brought me out of the womb?" (Meaning, why was I ever born?) "Oh, that I had perished and no eye had seen me! I would have been as though I had not been. I would be carried from the womb to the grave. Are not my days few? Cease! Leave me alone, that I may take a little comfort, Before I go to the place from which I shall not return, To the land of darkness and the shadow of death, without any order, Where even the light is like darkness" (Job 10:18-21 New King James).

Just like Job, we tend to desire to be all-alone when we get depressed. This is the worst thing to do. The only way to get back the cheerful heart is to get back with the people that can encourage you. And the BEST WAY to get back the cheerful heart, (the fastest way as well), is also biblical. When I say it's biblical, this means it's TRUTH! (Try it! Take me to task.) In the Book of Proverbs, the Book of wisdom, verse 11:25 says, "The one who blesses others is abundantly blessed; those who help others are helped" (The Message) The NIV Bible says, "he who refreshes (encourages) others will himself be refreshed."

Go out and be a blessing to others. Encourage someone who is down. Smile at strangers passing you by. Do some community volunteer work. I can assure you, you will feel a special touch when you do this. Your spirit will be lifted. It may be very tough to do this in the beginning, especially if you are down a little yourself. But it will work. "The one who blesses others is abundantly blessed …" Start blessing others and then look for your blessings. You will see them if you know how to look for them. Don't be like those people coming up to me on the beach. They look for just a minute, don't see it, and then go back to what they were doing. Start right now.

Uncover Your Talent

I enjoy sharing real stories about seeing the hand of God in events that I encounter each week. It is actually the things that I witness personally that inspire the lessons that I write. My desire is to encourage you in your walk with the Lord so that you too will see God's active hand in your daily walk. In this manner, you will begin to share your stories with others, which will in effect encourage others. Today I want to encourage you to dig up your talent if by some chance you've buried it. You may already be thinking, "Robby, how can I bury a talent? What do you mean by talent anyway?" I will address these questions in this lesson.

There is a parable taught by Jesus in the Bible called The Parable of the Talents. This story is told in Matthew 25: 14-30. Jesus told a very similar story in the Book of Luke, chapter 19, called "The Parable of the Ten Minas." If you read the two stories you will see how very close they are related to each other. The former story was told specifically to His disciples, and the latter was told to a crowd of people.

If you look up the word "talent" in Webster's Dictionary, you first see the definition for how the word was used in this parable. The definition reads: "1 a: any of several ancient units of weight, and b: a unit of value equal to the value of a talent of gold or silver." In the parable,

Jesus is teaching about how things will be when you pass from this life and you go before Him. In His illustration, He is the man traveling on a journey to a far country (heaven), and we are the servants. Jesus teaches, "For the kingdom of heaven is like a man traveling to a far country, who called his own servants and delivered his goods to them. And to one he gave five talents, to another two, and to another one, to each according to his own ability; and immediately he went on a journey" (Matthew 25: 14-15 NKJV).

Notice that the servants received the "goods" of the man traveling. We have received gifts/goods from the Lord. Do you know which "good" that you have been given? You have been delivered a gift according to your specific ability. God's Word tells us in the Book of Romans: "So we are to use our different gifts in accordance with the grace that God has given us. If our gift is to speak God's message, we should do it according to the faith that we have; if it is to serve, we should serve; if it is to teach, we should teach; if it is to encourage others, we should do so ..." (Romans 12:6-8 Good News Translation). Has your "gift" been uncovered yet? Hold on, there are three others: "if it is contributing to the needs of others, let him give generously; if it is leadership, let him govern diligently; if it is showing mercy, let him do it cheerfully" (Romans 12:8 NIV).

Which of the above goods have been delivered to you by the Man traveling to a far country? The Parable of the Talents goes on to say, "After a long time the master of those servants returned and settled accounts with them" (Matthew 25:19 NIV). There is a day when we will account for how we used our "goods." You may be thinking, "Robby, I heard that if I placed my trust in Jesus, the "Master" in the parable, that I wouldn't have to ever go before any judgment seat." Well, praise the Lord you won't be at the judgment seat to see whether you're getting into heaven or not, but the Bible says that we all will face the judgment of Christ: "For we must all appear before the judgment seat of Christ, that each one may receive what is due him for the things done while in the body, whether good or bad" (2 Corinthians 5:10 NIV). So I ask you, what do you think the Bible verse means when it says, "that each one may receive what is due him for the things done while in the body?"

The parable given by Jesus explains what it means. In Matthew 25 the Bible says, "The man who had received the five talents went at once and put his money to work and gained five more. So also, the one with the two talents gained two more. But the man who had received the one talent went off, dug a hole in the ground and hid his master's money" (Matthew 25:16-18). Is your gift being productive for His glory, or have you buried your gift, your God given talent?

This parable really has nothing to do with money, unless your gift covered in Romans 12 above is the gift of "contributing to the needs of others." Jesus goes on to teach, "The man who had received the five talents brought the other five. 'Master,' he said, 'you entrusted me with five talents. See, I have gained five more.' His master replied, 'Well done, good and faithful servant! You have been faithful with a few things; I will put you in charge of many things. Come and share your master's happiness!'" (Matthew 25:20-21). You may be thinking, "What could Jesus mean by placing one in 'charge of many things?'" In the Parable of the Ten Minas, the many things are being rulers of many cities.

There are different rewards when you get to heaven. Very much of your reward is based upon how you invest in your God given gift here on earth "while in the body." I remember several years ago when I first started seminary, I was teaching a middle school Sunday school class. I made mention to the class about the rewards in heaven, and an adult who was sitting in the class challenged my teaching in front of the group of young students. He said that heaven will be the same to all that enter. I just smiled at him but kept on teaching. It did bother me how he challenged me in front of the group, but I figure that he had the same vision of many that when we get to heaven; we just sit around like angels on clouds playing our harps and singing praises.

Jesus tells us in the Book of Matthew 6:19-20, "Do not store up for yourselves treasures on earth, where moth and rust destroy, and where thieves break in and steal. But store up for yourselves treasures in heaven, where moth and rust do not destroy, and where thieves do not break in and steal." So I ask you, if we can store up treasures, meaning many, how do we go about doing that? The Book of 2 John 1:8 warns us to: "Watch out that you do not lose what you have worked for, but that you may be rewarded fully." I could go on to give you many more reward verses, but I will conclude with the one found in the end. This is found in the very last chapter of the Bible, Revelation 22:12. Jesus says, "Behold, I am coming soon! My reward is with me, and I will give to everyone according to what he has done."

So, what have you done? The day I write this lesson is January 1, 2008. The beginning of a new year is always a good time for a challenge to start something new. Perhaps today is a good day to think about what the God-given gift to you, "your talent", is, and how you may begin to better invest it in the Kingdom. You may be thinking, "Robby, I'm not sure what my "talent" is. How do I find out for sure?" I say pray about it and ask the Lord to show you. Ask someone close to you what he or she believes your God-given gift is. Then go out and give some of your talent away to others. If it is encouraging, go out and encourage more; if it is teaching, go teach a Sunday school class, or start a small Bible study; if it is contributing to the needs of others, give. Jesus tells us in Luke 6:38 to: "Give, and it will be given to you. A good measure, pressed down, shaken together and running over, will be poured into your lap. For with the measure you use, it will be measured to you."

I mentioned in the beginning of my lesson that I like to share real stories that happen in my life. Just this Christmas season, I experienced just what I am teaching in this lesson. A few months ago this year, I received a note from a friend whom I have never met. We have corresponded by e-mail and postal mail, and we talked once on the phone, but we have never met. In our correspondence we have bonded as Christian brothers. He lives in Arizona. In his note to me, he said that he had come across an economic challenge and could use any gift that I could manage to give. I mailed him $100.00. It was a small gift that I intended to fully give away and not desire back. He soon sent me a note of gratitude.

Just before Christmas I received a letter from him. In the letter was a check for $150.00 and a note to me that blessed me. I immediately wanted to send the check back, but I kept reading his note. He said that perhaps I would come across someone in my ministry that could use the money this Christmas. I was touched, but I had no one in particular in mind. Here I sent $100 and received $150. I was beginning to see how God's economy worked. I began to pray about where to use the money.

Two days later I received an e-mail from a wonderful friend. She told me about an old high school classmate that had been diagnosed recently with cancer. I called my e-mailing friend on the phone and as we talked more she added that the illness had brought about such a financial burden on this dear family. My heart began to melt. In my spirit I knew now where the money was to be sent. My prayers were clearly answered. You may think, "Boy, Robby that sounds pretty neat beyond a coincidence." I say yeah, but hold on to your hat—there's more!

I mailed a card and placed the $150 in the card. I felt good because I was being obedient. I soon received a very heartwarming phone call from the family that I have not spoken to for over 32 years. They said that the card and the gift were very timely and they praised God for it. (Now remember that I had only $100 invested in this gift.) Over the holidays I went to my annual company Christmas party. Each year at the party my employer buys gifts for all the employees and their spouse/guest that attend the event. They wrap the gifts up, and we go one at a time to choose a gift. It's a gift swap, and when your turn comes, you either choose an unwrapped gift or "steal" an opened gift that someone has already opened. It's fun to watch.

This year they added a new twist. They wrapped a "mystery" gift that the person who received it couldn't open until the very end. We were told that it was either something good, or a good joke. I decided to go for the mystery gift even though the gifts available were very good. After all gifts were exchanged, they asked me to come to the front and open my "mystery" gift so all could see. I went up front and opened the package. The small box inside said, "Lump of coal." Everyone began to laugh very loud at the gift I ended up with. (I kind of turned red from embarrassment, but I was OK.) Then my boss' wife said, "Look inside the box." Sure enough inside was a lump of coal and when I brought it out of the box the crowd laughed even louder. Then I noticed attached to the bottom of the coal was—can you guess? It was a hundred dollar bill! I believe that our Lord has a good sense of humor.

You may be thinking, "Cute story Robby, but that was all just a neat coincidence." Maybe it was, maybe it wasn't? When you start seeing all the "coincidences" that I see each week, you may begin to realize that I am either one of the luckiest guys in the world, or there is something to all of these "coincidences" that happen. That is why the title of my first book is *Things Don't Just Happen*.

The Parable of the Talents told by Jesus ends by the master scolding the servant who buried his talent. The servant tried to reason with the master that he kept his gift hidden so that he could return it at the day of accounting. This did not please the master and the master said, "Take the talent away from him and give it to the one who has the ten talents. For everyone who has will be given more, and he will have an abundance. Whoever does not have, even what he has will be taken from him. And throw that worthless servant outside, into the darkness, where there will be weeping and gnashing of teeth" (Matthew 25:28-30).

Keeping your talent to yourself does not please the Lord. If it's been buried for a while, dig it up and put it to use. You too will begin to see God's economy work in your life. Here is a law of the Lord that you can bank on: "A generous man will prosper; he who refreshes others will himself be refreshed" (Proverbs 11:25).

This is a Test- This is Only a Test

Have you ever heard the phrase above? Sure you have. We hear it most often on the radio, and sometimes on the television. The message follows a sound, and then comes the following words: "This has been a test of the Emergency Broadcasting System. The broadcasters in your area in voluntary cooperation have developed this system to keep you informed in the event of an emergency. If this had been an actual emergency, the Attention Signal you just heard would have been followed by official information, news, or instructions …"

After hearing this message recently I wondered, have you been under a test (trial) recently? I think that I'm coming out of one myself. Does God test us? Wouldn't it be nice if He would make some sort of sound, like the emergency broadcast sound, just before we were about to go into a test so at least we would be a little prepared? I'm here to tell you today about the test (trial) that you may be going through. This is a test–this is only a test.

Most of us don't like test. I don't care for the "tests of life," nor do I like school tests. In my seminary classes today I still get pre-test jitters each time I sit down to take an exam. I almost have test anxiety each time; I'm afraid that I might choke and forget all of the information that

I have been cramming into my brain to prepare for the test. What I do like to hear from our teachers are the words "open book exam." Did you know that the test that you may be under right now is an open book exam? (The answers are found in your Bible.) That is A Good Word, but even open book exams can be very tough.

The Bible says in James 1:2-3, "Consider it pure joy, my brothers, whenever you face trials of many kinds, because you know that the testing of your faith develops perseverance. Perseverance must finish its work so that you may be mature and complete, not lacking anything" (NIV). Hmmm? The testing of your faith develops perseverance–now what does that mean? Let's look at some other translations. The New Living Translation says, "For when your faith is tested, your endurance has a chance to grow." The Message says, "You know that under pressure, your faith-life is forced into the open and shows its true colors." Now, perhaps that passage is beginning to have more meaning. Is my faith strong under this trial, or have I just thrown that "going to church thing" right out the window and I'm going to endure this "test" on my own?

You may be thinking now, "Robby, I'm not sure if the Lord does test us. He knows everything, right? Why would He test me if He knows if I'm going to pass or fail?"

My wife Julie, whom I love deeply, is a great schoolteacher. She teaches at a middle school close to home. As a teacher, she gives tests to her students. I know that she loves her students. During the school year, I get to know several of her students very well without ever meeting any of them by just listening to her tell me about them. Through her love, she really wants her students to learn the material taught and be able to apply it to their life. She also knows, before the test is given, who will pass the test and who will fail. Many times, tests are given to let the students know where their own efforts have placed them.

God works this way. He knows your heart and your true faith in His ability to watch after you. He already knows the results of your test–but do you? Proverbs 17:3 says, "The crucible for silver and the furnace for gold, but the Lord tests the heart" (NIV). Another great verse is Jeremiah 17:10: "I, the Lord, search the minds and test the hearts of people. I treat each of them according to the way they live, according to what they do"(Good News Translation). Just like I told you earlier, your test is an open Book test. I'm just uncovering some of the answers of your exam to help you out a little. You can find all of the answers yourself in the Course Book. I would like to encourage you to take advantage of the open Book test.

I truly believe that my calling is to encourage you during your test times. My desire is for you is to pass the test, keep the faith, and most importantly be prepared for the final exam. The test in front of you may be one of the toughest that you have ever gone through. But sometimes that's just what we have to do when we are in a tough test—go through it. When Moses was leading the Israelites out of Egypt, God gave many tests to His people. One of the tests was the desert itself. Once they were in, many wanted to go back. But the only way through the test of the desert was to go through it. The blessings were on the other side.

My prayer for you is to get through your test and find the blessings on the other side. In the Book of Deuteronomy 8:16, the Bible speaks of one of the tests of His people in the desert. The open Book also tells us why the test was given: "who fed you in the wilderness with manna, which your fathers did not know, that He might humble you and that He might test you, to do you good in the end" (NKJ). The Bible tells us here that the test was to "do you good in the end." Learning and growing has always involved tests. Sometimes learning and growing has to involve a little discipline. Why might your "test" be a little discipline? "because the Lord disciplines those he loves ..." (Proverbs 3:12).

God loves you! He loves you so much that He gave His one and only Son to help you in your daily test: "Come to me, all you who are weary and burdened, and I will give you rest" (Matthew 11:28 NIV). But most importantly, His Son came in order for you to pass the final exam that I wrote about earlier: "to do you good in the end." Jesus said, "For my Father's will is that everyone who looks to the Son and believes in him shall have eternal life, and I will raise him up that last day" (John 6:40 NIV). That last day—there's your final exam. That day is when your test will no longer just be a test. Hopefully you will only hear the emergency broadcast signal and not the actual emergency broadcast message that day. The signal will be a trumpet call: "and with the trumpet call of God, and the dead in Christ will rise first. After that, we who are still alive and are left will be caught up together with them in the clouds to meet the Lord in the air. And so we will be with the Lord forever" (1 Thessalonians 4:16-17).

If this had been an actual emergency, the Trumpet Sound that you just heard would have been followed by the official rapture of the Church.

Don't Miss Third Base

In high school I played several sports. In all four years of my time in high school I hardly ever went home as soon as the school day ended. This kept me plenty busy. This was good for me. I have learned that keeping busy makes a person more productive in all areas. This is true in any age of life.

I had a recent conversation with a student enrolled in Kennesaw State University. He told me about the two part time jobs that he was holding while he managed taking four classes at the University. I said, "Man, you need to let up a little, don't you?" He went on to explain to me that he was making the best grades that he has ever made. It was the discipline of managing a full schedule that allowed him to perform at his potential. The Bible says in Proverbs 12:11: "Hard work means prosperity; only fools idle away their time" (New Living Translation). Prosperity can mean good grades, good performance in your job, or being a good stay at home mom.

One of the sports that I participated in during the spring was baseball. The first day of spring was last week (at the writing of this lesson), so I figured that I would toss in a baseball lesson. It seems only appropriate since the Braves break spring training at the end of this week.

During my junior year of high school, I played first base. I am left-handed, so that's where most of us lefties get positioned. I've written an earlier lesson about my love for running track in school. (I was much better in track than baseball). I was better known on the baseball team as the best base runner just because of my speed. If we ever needed a run to be scored from one of the bases, the coach tried to get me on base.

We just happened to be involved in an important region game, and we were in one of those situations where we needed a run to win the game. The game was tied, and we were in the bottom of the last inning with two outs already. We were the home team, so a run scored in our half of the inning would mean a win for us. It was my turn at bat, and I placed a nice bunt down the third base line and beat the throw to first. So far, so good. On the second pitch to my good friend at the plate, Lloyd, I stole second. (Like I said, I was fast.)

So here I am, on second base, with two outs. The crowd was really going wild. We had the fastest runner in the school on second base (me), and our best hitter at the plate, Lloyd. I'm pretty much in the spotlight now. I liked it. I looked the part, jumping all around at second base just showing that opposing team how fast I was. All we needed was just a hit, and I would score. I was pumped!

The next pitch came and sure enough, Lloyd hit a grounder past the third baseman right in front of me. Now I'm flying with all I've got. I rounded third base and headed home, full steam ahead. I slid in on home plate, and the crowd went wild! All of my teammates ran out of the dugout and began to hug me. We were feeling great! The game was over and we won... or did we?

You see, as I walked toward the bench to get my stuff, I noticed that the opposing team has not left the field. My coach was still standing in the third base coach box. The crowd suddenly got quiet as they wondered what was going on. Then one of my fellow teammates asked me, "Robby, you touched third base on your way home, didn't you?" I said, "Of course, I did." I've been playing baseball a long time. I knew that you had to touch ALL bases to get home. I even yelled out to the umpire, "I touched third base!"

Well, the opposing pitcher told the umpire they were appealing the "touching" of third base, and then he threw the ball to the third baseman. The umpire yelled as loud as I ever heard one yell, "He's OUT!" We lost the game. ***Today's Good Word of encouragement is to tell you not to miss third base if you want to reach home.***

Several years ago, I was sitting in the kitchen of my older sister, Sherryl. We were discussing how I was beginning to feel the new call of the Lord in my life. Then she asked me, "How do you know that you are going to heaven?" I began to explain that I knew with certainty because I was a good person. I did all sorts of nice things for people, and I had a loving heart. I then told her about how I went to church and enjoyed the things about church. Don't all of these answers seem convincing to you? Doesn't it seem to you that I had all of the bases covered in order to reach home plate (heaven)? You see, I missed third base again!

First base is the answer about being a good person. We all feel at one time that since we are "a good person" we deserve to go into heaven. A loving God would let us into heaven if we were a good person, wouldn't He? Can't we do "good works" to get into heaven? No! The Bible says in Galatians 2:16: "...yet we know that no one is justified by the works of the law but by faith in Jesus Christ. And we have believed in Christ Jesus, so that we might be justified by faith in Christ and not by the works of the law, because by the works of the law no human being will be justified" (Holman Christian Standard Bible). Also in the Book of Ephesians 2:8-9 the Bible says: "For it is by grace you have been saved, through faith—and it is not from yourselves, it is the gift of God—not by works, so that no one can boast" (NIV). Therefore, just getting on first base doesn't get you home.

Second base is the answer about attending church. I love how my Pastor says, "Just because you stand in your garage, doesn't make you a car." Neither will going to church necessarily make you a born-again Christian. Now, going to church is good and needed in one's life. (Read my lesson *Home Field Advantage*.) Going to church is like reaching second base; you should touch second base on your way to home plate.

The Bible says in Hebrews 10:25: "Let us not give up meeting together, as some are in the habit of doing, but let us encourage one another—and all the more as you see the Day approaching" (NIV). You'll get great encouragement being on second base. I heard the fans cheering me on toward home plate while I was on second base. Go to church. Feel encouraged to reach home plate yourself.

Like my story above, third base must be touched to reach home plate (heaven). You must ask the Lord Jesus to live within your heart. A personal relationship with Jesus is third base. "Everyone who calls on the name of the Lord will be saved" (Romans 10:13 NIV). And "That if you confess with your mouth, 'Jesus is Lord,' and believe in your heart that God raised him from the dead, you will be saved" (Romans 10:9). Don't miss third base!

Many people, unfortunately, will miss third base. They will be telling the umpire (Jesus as Judge) that, "I touched all the bases, look at what I did in your name." And the umpire will say, "You're Out! In the Bible, the Lord Jesus explains it this way: "Not everyone who says to me, 'Lord, Lord,' will enter the kingdom of heaven, but only he who does the will of my Father who is in heaven. Many will say to me on that day, 'Lord, Lord, did we not prophesy in your name, and in your name drive out demons and perform many miracles?' Then I will tell them plainly, 'I never knew you. Away from me, you evildoers!" (Matthew 7: 21-23). In other words, "You're Out!"

Last year, I paid a visit to my old baseball coach, Ron Causey, who was coaching third base that day (I love Coach Causey). He remembered the game as well, even though it was over 31 years ago. He told me, "Robby, I was never upset with you about that. It was my job as a third base coach to make sure that you touched third base. I should have done my job and called you back to touch the base when you ran by." That comment did make me feel better even after all of those years.

Today my job is to be your "third base coach." I won't let you miss third base. I'm standing here waving you around, and I'm calling your name toward home plate. But at the same time, I'm pointing toward third base so you will know to touch it. If you run by, I will call you back to touch it—just read my next lesson.

A Good Word

The title of this lesson is kind of catchy, don't you think? In case you don't know already, the title is also the name of my website ministry. The idea for the name of my web site is both from my wife, Julie, and Pastor Johnny Hunt of First Baptist Church Woodstock, Georgia. Often during Pastor Johnny's sermons, he will stop and say; "Now that was a good Word!" He normally makes this reflection after reading from God's Word.

Today I have a good word for you. The inspiration for this lesson came this morning from my daily Bible reading. I'm sure that I have read this verse before, but today it sank in a little differently. It pretty much sums up my ministry. In the Book of Proverbs 12:25 the Bible says, "Anxiety weighs down the human heart, but a good word cheers it up" (New Revised Standard Version). I pray that each lesson that I write will be a good word to cheer your heart up.

In today's fast paced world there are plenty of places for you to receive your daily dose of anxiety. It all may start early if the first thing that you do each day is to turn on the news. I personally don't do this on purpose. Many of my friends have kidded me on certain days about not knowing what the latest news story is. I just don't go there. I get my cup of coffee and head to my quiet room. This usually includes my television set. But instead of the daily news report, I watch a recording of praise and worship videos. There are a couple of shows that I recommend that you set your devise to record. One is called *Worship Videos* and the other is called *Creation Scapes*. Both of these programs show video of God's wonderful creation as praise music is played.

After my first cup of coffee, my eyes finally adjust to where I can read God's Word. This is what is important! The news that you read in the paper or hear on the radio may affect you today or tomorrow, but Jesus tells us, "do not worry about tomorrow, for tomorrow will worry about itself. Each day has enough trouble of its own" (Matthew 6:34 NIV). Isn't that so true today? Each day does have enough trouble on its own without you getting all upset on how things will turn out. The thing that is most important to you and to your family is what Jesus says in the verse just before this passage.

Above, I wrote from the Book of Proverbs about how anxiety weighs down the human heart. Most anxiety comes from worry: worry about jobs, worry about health, worry about relationships, worry about the future. Jesus addresses this in Matthew 6:25: "Therefore I tell you, do not worry about your life, what you will eat or drink; or about your body, what you will wear." I understand that this is not easy to do. But, the good word I have for you today is how to take each day on with an attitude of faith. What I am about to tell you REALLY WORKS! I've tried it and I'm here to testify.

Turn to Matthew 6:33 and get your highlight pen out. Read this and mark it. Memorize it! Jesus says, "But seek first his kingdom and his righteousness, and all these things will be given to you as well." Seek God and His ways first and foremost in your life, and then all other things will just fall into place for you. Remember that God's ways may not be your ways. But God's ways are better. His plans for you are where you want to be. God tells us in Jeremiah 29:11: "For I know the plans I have for you, … plans to give you hope and a future."

The Bible also tells us that if you seek first His kingdom and His righteousness that the Lord WILL fulfill His purpose for you. Knowing your purpose will give you all the daily inspiration that you may need to make it to the next day. The Bible shares this promise in Psalms 138: 7-8: "Though I walk in the midst of trouble, you preserve my life; you stretch out your hand against the anger of my foes, with your right hand you save me. The Lord will fulfill his purpose for me; your love, O Lord, endures forever—do not abandon the works of your hands."

To reach your purpose, you must make sure that you have friends that help you move toward fulfilling your purpose—friends that have a positive outlook on life, and friends that have the same faith and values that you do. The people that you are around, the things that you read, the shows that you watch, and the music that you listen to, all have a tremendous influence on your daily walk. These things can also either add to the heaviness of your heart to weigh it down, as the Proverbs say, or these things can lift your spirits high, knowing and believing the promises of God. Choose your "things" that move you toward fulfilling your purpose.

I encourage you to start your day in the Word of God. Today to get started, turn to 2 Peter 1 and read verses 3 through 11. In this passage, the Apostle Peter shares with us the promise of our ability to never fall. This is good news! Good News that will not only affect you today, but news that will affect you eternally—and that's a long time.

Early Warning Detection

As I sat down to begin writing this lesson, I flipped my calendar over to the next month (the day I write this is March 1, 2008). It was refreshing to change from the month long snow picture to the current spring-like photograph on my wall calendar. I am excited that the warm weather season is approaching, but with this transition in weather patterns comes occasional severe storms as new cold fronts plow through.

This past Tuesday was one of those transitional weather days. If you know me at all, you will know that bad weather with high winds scares me. A severe storm blew through here just before daylight. The whole house made a creaking sound as the front edge of the storm hit our house. I scooted down to my basement to ask a prayer of protection. You may say, "Well, Robby, if you had great faith, you would have prayed while upstairs for that protection." You have a good point, and I have a good friend named Anthony who always reminds me about Psalms 139:16: "you saw me before I was born. The days allotted to me had all been recorded in your book, before any of them ever began" (Good News Translation). So even though my appointed day of death is already set, I choose not to hasten it by sitting upstairs in severe storms, nor will I ride my motorcycle without a helmet.

Upon my return from the basement, I noticed cars in the street in front of my driveway were coming to a rapid stop. This was unusual because the traffic light is hundreds of yards away. As I watched the cars go by in the dark and pouring rain, I noticed that they would come to a hard brake in front of my house and then turn around and come back by in the other direction in a couple of minutes. I figured that a tree must be down across the road.

As soon as the lightning stopped, I put on my raincoat and went out into the dark with my flashlight to see what was causing the problem. Sure enough, a huge pine tree had fallen across the road, and there was no way to get by. There was a car already stuck in the mud in my front yard, attempting to turn around. It was about 6:30 AM, and the traffic was just building. I knew in a few minutes there would be many cars coming by and trying to turn around in my yard. I went back into my house to ask my wife to call someone about the tree.

As I went back outside, I could hear sirens in all directions, so I knew that my street was not an isolated closing. I walked down to the neighborhood entrance just below my house and started waving my flashlight and arms, as a car would approach. One car at a time would come by, and the driver would stop to ask me what was wrong. I would warn each person of the hazard ahead and give advice on how to get out of the situation safely without getting stuck in the mire. There was plenty of room for an easy turn-around at that location, so the people would thank me for my guidance and go the direction that I advised them to travel.

Most people would stop and ask me about my warning as I waved my arms. These people would receive clear instructions on ways to avoid a certain hazard. But did you guess that some people would see me standing there waving my arms and flashlight but choose to keep on going toward the hazard? I would have to step out of their way in order not to get hit because they were dead set on moving in their directed course of muck and mire. By now you may be thinking, "Robby, I can see a lesson developing from this story. Did this really happen?" Yes, it did.

Like I said, most people stopped and thanked me for giving them a clear understanding of the hazard that they could avoid, but not one person who passed my warning stopped to say, "Thanks for trying to warn me." They would just drive back by with mud covering their car from being stuck in the mire. They were too embarrassed to even glance my way. Today, as you read this lesson, I want you to imagine that I am in front of you waving my arms with my flashlight. Perhaps you may be moving toward a muck and mire hazard ...

Hopefully, you can say, "Robby I'm doing good. I don't need any warning sign." I say praise the Lord for that, but let me also add a line from the flight attendant when you are first seated on an airplane. You remember the line—"In the unlikely event of a water landing, you can use your seat cushion as a flotation device." I say, in the unlikely event of getting stuck in mire, and to keep from heading that way, here is A Good Word to keep your path clear: "Your word is a lamp to my feet and a light for my path" (Psalms 119:105 NIV). The Bible, God's Word, is your early warning detection system. You see, there is power in God's Word. The Bible says, "our gospel came to you not simply with words, but also with power, with the Holy Spirit and with deep conviction" (1 Thessalonians 1:5). This passage says the Bible is more than just words and stories. It has real living power to convict and change. It can give you very clear early warning signs to keep you from the slippery mucky paths that your enemy desires for you to travel: "Therefore their path will become slippery; they will be banished to darkness and there they will fall" (Jeremiah 23:12).

You may ask, "Robby, were there warning signs in the Bible that should have been obvious to certain people?" There were MANY, and not all warning signs were given to evil people. Sometimes I am asked if I think that the Bible has any mistakes in it. I say, "Absolutely! There are plenty of mistakes, and don't you make one like Adam and Eve, David, and Solomon who chose not to follow the commands of our Lord, the inerrant Word of God." The warning that comes to my mind first is to one of the Bible's strongest believers and followers of Christ Jesus. The warning was given to Simon Peter, one of the disciples of Jesus. Jesus warns, "Simon, Simon, Satan has asked to sift you as wheat. But I have prayed for you, Simon, that your faith may not fail." This is in the story when Peter told Jesus that he would follow Him no matter what happened, even "to prison and to death." Jesus replied, "I tell you Peter, before the rooster crows today, you will deny three times that you know me" (Luke 22: 31-34). Satan desires to sift you and me away from following and obeying Jesus. He uses his device of compromise as a weapon for our destruction.

You might ask, "Robby, explain this 'compromise' a little bit further." It is generally very easy for you and me to say no to the large temptations of sin (missing the mark established by God). For example, the eighth commandment says, "You shall not steal"(Deuteronomy 5:19). You probably think to yourself that following this one is easy. But what happens is that we fall, one little compromise at a time. I'm sure that the local college professor who recently was charged with theft didn't ever imagine using a state government credit card for over $300,000.00 for personal charges. She probably just compromised on that very first charge, thinking that the state owed it to her because she worked overtime one day. The next charge was easier to make, and so it grew.

Satan's device of compromise is the same today as it was with Adam and Eve. God's command was, "You must not eat fruit from the tree that is in the middle of the garden, and you must not touch it, or you will die." Satan knew which tree was forbidden, but he asked Eve, "Did God really say, 'You must not eat from any tree in the garden?'" (Genesis 3:1-3). He still likes to place that doubt in our minds today that just a little compromise is OK. Slowly we're drawn into a trap of muck and mire. It's kind of like being on a diet to lose weight. You think, "I can just eat one Oreo cookie and satisfy my sweet craving." So you eat one and then think, "Well I've already blown my diet now, I might as well eat the whole pack."

This deceptive snare worked the same for Peter back in the story of his denial, as Jesus had warned. The first compromise was small when Peter was first asked if he had been with Jesus: "But he denied it. "I don't know or understand what you are talking about," he said, and went out into the entryway" (Mark 14:68). This was just a small compromise for Peter. He may have thought to himself, "I didn't do anything wrong. I didn't deny Jesus." But look where the first small compromise lead to: The third time that he was asked if he was a follower of Jesus: "He began to call down curses on himself, and he swore to them, 'I don't know this man you're talking about.' Immediately the rooster crowed ..." (Mark 14:71-72).

When you and I begin to compromise, we, too, are denying Jesus. Jesus says, "If you love me, you will obey what I command" (John 14:15). You find out what He commands by reading your Bible. So here I am standing in front of you, waving my flashlight. Is there anything in your life going on now that you've compromised just a little? Just as in the example in my storm story above, I'm standing in front of a wide area for you to easily turn around in now. The definition of repent actually includes the words "to turn." Don't go any further! Here is your early warning, because ahead there is a roadblock that only leads to slippery mud and mire. Stop and roll down your window. I know the way out of this mess. The Bible says, "God is faithful; he will not let you be tempted beyond what you can bear. But when you are tempted, he will also provide a way out so that you can stand up under it" (1 Corinthians 10:13).

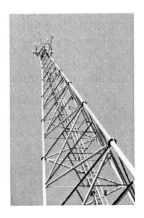

Communication Tower Bombs

I have always enjoyed sports. I grew up in a great neighborhood where I had several friends who lived near by. We would often get together and play different sporting events in a field not far from my house. I don't believe that the youth of today get together to do these kinds of things much any more. Perhaps the age of video games replaced the neighborhood ball games.

I believe that athletic competitions teach many lessons of life. One such lesson came to mind a couple of weeks ago while I was watching the Super Bowl football game on TV. Even though the playing arena in the Super Bowl is supposed to be a neutral field, often times like this past game, one team is much closer to the event. This was the case with the Pittsburgh Steelers. Their fans were much closer than the fans of Seattle; therefore, Pittsburgh had the "home field" advantage.

The big home field advantage in a football game is the noise made by the fans. The Atlanta Falcon fans are good about doing this. What happens is, when the visiting team has the ball, the fans yell so loudly that the players on the line of scrimmage cannot hear the plays called from the line by the quarterback. Without knowing the play, the players have no direction. This tactic can actually help defeat a team.

You see, even though the player on the offensive line is fully equipped, fully trained, and ready for the fight, if he can't hear the play, he doesn't have any direction. If the communication link between the quarterback and the rest of the team is not functioning properly, defeat is certain. The head coach sends the play to the quarterback, and the quarterback communicates the play to the team in the game. Who might be our "quarterback" in church? Is your communication link working to properly hear the play called? Are you hearing the play to know your direction?

In a war, the first thing that an enemy attacks is the communication towers. Without the ability to properly communicate, defeat is certain no matter how many weapons that you possess. You may be on a battleship poised just off of the coast full of bombs ready for launch. If the ship cannot communicate with the commander giving directions to the targets, it is pretty much a useless piece of floating metal with no direction.

My point is this: you may be full of knowledge and have all the tools to perform, but if you don't have communication with the commander or the head coach, you have no direction in your life. You can be going through the motions, but if you are following your own playbook, you really have no direction. You can carry your Bible, you can attend church every time the doors open, you can have all the tools and potential, but if your communication tower is not working properly, you are just like the football player on the field who can't hear the play. He's fully dressed for battle with hours of training behind him, but he can't hear the play and he doesn't know the direction to go.

If the football fans have figured it out, if the military leaders have figured it out, then who do you think knows that the way to defeat you is to destroy your communication tower? The Bible says, "be strong in the Lord and in his mighty power. Put on the full armor of God so that you can take your stand against the devil's schemes" (Ephesians 6:10-11 NIV). One of the devil's schemes is to plant bombs under your communication towers.

You have several communication towers. The big one links you with the Lord through prayer. How often are you using it? My cell phone has a program called call log. I can scroll through this log to see whom I have called in the last several entries. If your body had a call log scroll button that I could punch to see a list of your last several outbound calls, how many times would a call to God show up?

Communication to the Lord is essential for your direction. This is God's purpose for your life. Prayer works! The Lord communicates through prayer. The Lord works through prayer. Do you need any help in any of your direction here now? The Bible says, "This is the confidence we have in approaching God: that if we ask anything according to his will, he hears us. And if we know that he hears us- whatever we ask- we know that we have what we asked of him" (1 John 5:14-15).

James 5:13 tells us: "Is any one of you in trouble? He should pray." You may be thinking, "Well Robby, I did pray for a while but nothing happened. God knows my needs. Why should I keep praying?" I say look at Luke 18:1. The Bible says, "Then Jesus told his disciples a parable to show them that they should always pray and not give up." In the following verses Jesus describes a lady going to a judge over and over again. The judge finally gives in saying," ... yet because this widow keeps bothering me, I will see that she gets justice, so that she won't eventually wear me out with her coming!"" (Luke 18:5). The Apostle Paul goes on to tell us in 1 Thessalonians 5:17 to:

"... pray continually" (NIV) or to, "Pray without ceasing" (KJV). God does know our needs, but He wants us to ask Him. The Bible says in James 4:2, "You do not have, because you do not ask God." God knew that the prophet Elijah wanted to show the people a sign from Him. (God knew it!) But He didn't do the signs until Elijah prayed about it and asked Him. The Bible says, "Elijah was a man just like us. He prayed earnestly that it would not rain, and it did not rain on the land for three and a half years. Again he prayed, and the heavens gave rain, and the earth produced its crops" (James 5:17-18).

Has the enemy planted a communication bomb under your tower? Is he successful in having the background noise in your life so loud that you can't hear the Lord's call on your playing field? I mentioned earlier that you have several communication towers. The tower that I am most vulnerable to is my communication tower to my family. (The people that I love the most!) The enemy knows that if he plants a precision bomb under that tower of mine, it also disrupts my main communication tower to God. Has he used that scheme on you?

I asked a dear Christian Brother friend of mine where he is most vulnerable to the enemy's communication tower bombs. His answer was, "Unconfessed sin." This was a powerful statement. Could this be the enemy's scheme against you? Listen to this awesome Bible verse. Psalms 66:18 says, "If I had cherished sin in my heart, the Lord would not have listened" (NIV). Please don't let your opponent use this scheme against you. You WANT the Lord to hear your prayers. The Bible says, "If we confess our sins, he is faithful and just and will forgive us our sins and purify us from all unrighteousness" (1John 1:9). This is a good tower repairing verse.

Talk to God. Pray often. Start off small if need be; just talk to Him. Give Him your thanksgiving and praise. Then ask Him to meet your needs and the needs of your friends and family. He wants to have communication with you. Prayer works! "I call on the Lord in my distress, and he answers me" (Psalms 120:1).

When you are outside of church or any other Christian gathering, you are at an away game. You may not be able to hear the signals of the quarterback because of all the noise and background activity going on. That's the enemy's plan. Call time out. Go into the locker room by yourself or with your team and communicate with the Lord through prayer. Then be still. Listen for answers of direction in your heart. He will give you the plays (direction) to have victory in the game.

Is Your Check Engine Light On?

My favorite time to write the web lessons is Saturday mornings before the sun comes up. I actually look forward to getting up every morning extra early just to spend some time in prayer and in the Word of God. It's during these times that I pray for you specifically.

This happens to be one of those early Saturday mornings. I'm pouring my second cup of coffee, and I'm saying, "Lord, I need Your inspiration for my web lesson this morning." As the comedian Bill Engvall of the Blue Collar Comedy Tour says, "Here's your sign."

This morning I am to go exchange a loaner car from the local car dealership and pick up my wife's car. The warning light that is shown above has been displayed on the dash panel of Julie's car, so hopefully the dealership has corrected the problem. We have had some problems with this pesky little symbol. The symbol has stayed on more than it has stayed off in this car. (I pray that they finally fixed the problem today.)

Each time that we've taken the car in for repair to have the symbol reset, it's usually been for minor things like a leaking gas cap or a loose vacuum hose. This being the case, we've almost come to ignore the symbol, but this may not be a wise thing. You see, today's car engines are very sophisticated pieces of engineering; the symbol is a warning sign that something is just not right. If the symbol is completely ignored long enough, the death of my car is certain.

Is your internal "check engine light" on? (You are a pretty significant piece of engineering.) Neat thing–I looked up Webster's Dictionary meaning of the word "symbol." Here is EXACTLY what one of the definitions states: "4: an object or act representing something in the unconscious mind that has been repressed." Want to know more neat stuff about Webster's definition of this word? In the on-line Webster definition it says, "–more at DEVIL" with a link to the definition of devil. Don't believe me, do you? Try it!

The definition above says an act representing something in the unconscious mind that has been repressed. What possibly can you be ignoring (repressing) in the unconscious mind (your spirit)? What does the devil have to do with this? Is it possible that we have an internal "symbol" that says, "Check Spirit." I say you should. This internal warning symbol is called the Holy Spirit. By God's grace we are given this Spirit when we become believers of Jesus Christ as our Lord.

Can you recall being somewhere or doing something that you just didn't feel right about doing? This is your internal "check engine" light coming on. The choice then becomes yours. Just like the check engine symbol in my wife's car, I can ignore it, or I can fix it. Ignore it long enough and failure is certain. The Bible says in Romans 8:5. "Those who live according to the sinful nature have their minds set on what that nature desires; but those who live in accordance with the Spirit have their minds set on what the Spirit desires" (NIV). What does the Spirit desire? The Spirit desires to please God.

The following is what the Bible tells us will happen when we decide to do right when that "Check Spirit" symbol lights up: "the mind controlled by the Spirit is life and peace" (Romans 8:6). Life and peace– that sounds pretty good. What is my alternative if I repress (ignore) the "Check Spirit" light? The Bible says in the same passage above: "The mind of a sinful man is death …" Now call me narrow- minded, but I like the sound of life and peace a lot better.

You may be thinking right now, "Now Robby, this is not one of your 'make me feel good' uplifting lessons." I know; I've struggled a little writing this. But what is MOST important to me is that you are a reader of my lessons–at least this lesson, and if you receive what I say here, your life will be so much better. The Word of God promises life and peace if the Spirit controls you. That is A Good Word!

Today we are bombarded so much with liberal TV shows, magazine ads, and even the news. I'm concerned that your warning light may come on, and you just repress it because of all of the junk fuel that you may have been using to fill your spiritual fuel tank. You may just ignore the warning symbol until it just burns itself out. At least check out the Owner's Manual if your light has been on. See what the Book says about your warning symbol. I have limited mechanical skills, and if I were reading your car manual, I wouldn't be much help. But I can give you great insight with your Owner's Manual (your Bible). I'm certain if you read through it yourself, you will be able to know how to make the repair so the warning light will reset itself.

Bad fuel in your car over time causes the fuel injectors to clog, and your engine will lose much of its capable performance. The injectors can become clogged, and the check engine light will light up. Your spiritual engine will do the same thing.

I've seen this happen in the church. Members will attend worship and Sunday school for several weeks and receive good fuel into their spiritual fuel tank. In speaking with them, it seems that they believe that things are going well for them and have a better sense of their purpose. They get a good tune up, filled with the best fuel available (God's Fuel) and then sometimes drive away from church for several weeks at a time.

Then what happens is they keep filling up week after week with the world's fuel. They think that they are doing OK because their engine keeps running. (Not knowing all along that their fuel ports are clogging up.) Suddenly they find themselves in a compromising situation, and their "check engine" light comes on. They have to decide (free will): Do I do something to correct the "check engine," or do I just ignore it and hopefully it will just turn itself off?

I have seen the results of the ones that just ignore the warning symbol. Breakdown is certain. Several make it back to the Good Gas station limping and sputtering as they pull in. They receive a strong dose of injector cleaner, "because our gospel came to you not simply with words, but also with power, with the Holy Spirit and with deep conviction" (1 Thessalonians 1:5). But unfortunately, the others stay away. I have passed by them on the sides of the road with their hoods lifted.

Today, I want to encourage you to stay in tune with your internal "check engine" light. Don't ignore the symbol if it gives you a warning. If you're not sure what to do when the warning is activated, pour some of this injector cleaner (God's Word) into your spiritual fuel tank …

It's Always Easier To Do Nothing!

Today's message is one that we all need to be reminded of from time to time. This goes especially for me. It's OK for you to think, "Robby wrote this message to himself, so I will read on to see what he deals with at times." You see, from time to time I begin to get a lot of things on my plate–my work, my school classes, my ministry, my family, and it becomes a little over-whelming. (Do you ever feel this way?) I begin to think to myself, "Boy, am I busy! I need to cut back on some things. Do I really need to spend that extra time in ministry for the Lord? Am I really making any difference? It sure would be easier if I would just focus on family and work, and just go to church service on Sunday. That one hour per week in worship service is plenty enough service for the Lord, isn't it? Why, that's much better than most folks give."

This reminds me of a story that happened a few weeks ago. I went to meet a business prospect near his business and he decided to meet at Waffle House for a cup of coffee. The meeting started late morning, so when I finished my presentation, my prospect left, and by then it was lunchtime. I super-enjoy Waffle House waffles, but I normally don't eat there except for breakfast. I looked at the menu and ordered a bowl of "The Best Chili in the World, Bert's Chili." Well to me, it's not the best. As a matter of fact, that day the chili served was just lukewarm. I only took a few bites and decided that's all of Bert that I could handle. Nobody really likes things served lukewarm, do they?

So I have to ask myself, "Is my service to the Lord ever lukewarm? Is lukewarm service for the Lord OK with Him? Surely He understands all that I have going on? As long as I attend service each Sunday and give my money, lukewarm is better than cold, isn't it?" Well–No.

Jesus answers my thoughts in the Book of Revelation, 3:15-16: "I know your deeds, that you are neither cold nor hot. I wish you were either one or the other! So, because you are lukewarm–neither hot nor cold–I am about to spit you out of my mouth" (NIV). Lukewarm service is not what He desires from me or from you. When we tend to be lukewarm, we just go through the motions. Our walk with the Lord may send confusing messages to those non-believers around us in school and our work. The non-believers do watch us! They know that we attend church on Sunday but more importantly, they also know the way we act and the things that we do during the week. Our actions of lukewarm discipleship can cause more harm than it would if we were just cold about our faith.

You may ask, "Robby, how do I keep from being lukewarm? If you struggle with it, how do you fight it off?" I keep believing the next passage in Revelation. Jesus goes on to tell us, "Here I am! I stand at the door and knock. If anyone hears my voice and opens the door, I will come in and eat with him, and he with me. To him who overcomes, I will give the right to sit with me on my throne, just as I overcame and sat down with my Father on his throne" (Revelation 3:20-21). I overcome by listening for His voice. I try to keep the door open for Him so He doesn't have to knock on my door. I do this by staying involved in a ministry for His glory. Many times I don't feel like serving Him because I am tired, but let me tell you A Good Word! The Bible says, "A generous man will prosper; he who refreshes others will himself be refreshed" (Proverbs 11:25).

Believe this verse! It is so true! Each and EVERY time that I have felt tired and uninspired to go to do a ministry for His glory, I have come back refreshed and full of energy. I challenge you to get involved in some sort of ministry to serve others in His name. This can be in the form of teaching a Sunday school class to young children, serving by visiting elders in their home or nursing home, cooking a meal for a family that has lost a loved one, sitting next to someone in the school cafeteria that may seem alone, volunteering for a service organization, writing notes of encouragement to friends going through tough times, listening to a co-worker who needs to share. You can make a difference in someone's life even though you may not think that you have something to offer. The Bible says that, "A cheerful look brings joy to the heart, and good news gives health to the bones" (Proverbs 15:30). You can bring joy to another's heart, and your smile and encouragement can actually add health to his innermost being.

I have a dear friend named Debbie. She is a wonderful servant for the Lord, even though she is going through a terrible illness. She could choose to stay at home and be upset with the trial that she is under. It would be so easy for her to just do nothing, but she has decided that this is her ministry. During each visit to the doctor she shares her love for the Lord with the staff and to other patients as they receive their medications. She even takes treats that have notes of encouragement attached with her to hand out. Her faith has impacted many others because they wonder why she is so full of joy even though she is fighting an illness. Debbie is a model to me, who follows the teaching of Peter, who says,

> "Always be prepared to give an answer to everyone who asks
> you to give the reason for the hope that you have" (1 Peter 3:15).

Today I want to encourage you to listen for His voice and open the door of your purpose. When you feel that tug to get involved, move forward. Any delays in your actions will be followed by another voice that says, "You're a good person just by thinking you should get involved, but someone else will do a much better job. Just do nothing because you really don't have the time." Don't believe that lie! I pray at that very moment you remember this lesson and you think, "It's always easier to do nothing. But that's not me." Be a light of dawn for others to see hope. As you travel down that path shining your light for others, your own path will even get brighter. The Bible says, "The path of the righteous is like the light of dawn, which shines brighter and brighter until full day" (Proverbs 4:18). Amen.

Open but Closed

This past week, I made an after dinner trip to get an ice cream cone at the local ice cream shop. I recently received an envelope with coupons inside for four free ice creams. That was my "reward" for doing right, even though I was tempted to do wrong. You see, on my last visit, when I received my double chocolate chunk, it was all melted and soft as mush. I went back to the window to complain, but the long line of folks really didn't want me to cut into their wait. After going on a special trip and paying about $3.00 for a melted mess, I wanted to walk up to the front and throw my purchase against the window in protest. That would have felt good for a moment, but I knew that it wasn't the right thing to do.

I write this short story to encourage you, and me, to do the right thing when we get upset about things that don't go our way. Our world is full of the big challenges that we will face, and we shouldn't let the small things like this, or rude people, affect our walk and witness. The Bible says, "Do not repay evil with evil or insult with insult, but with blessing, because to this you were called so that you may inherit a blessing" (1 Peter 3:9 NIV). In other words, we are to do the right thing and let God take care of any wrongs done to us. If I had splattered my melted good all over the front of that shop like I wanted to, my witness would have been very poor. What if one of my Sunday school students was in that long line? But I ask you, how could I "inherit a blessing" here?

There are about three places in the Bible that speaks about the Lord providing a double portion back in return for being obedient to Him: "the Lord made him prosperous again and gave him twice as much as he had before" (Job 42:10). I drove home upset that I was wronged, but the next morning I felt better, and I wrote a kind e-mail to the home office of the chain of ice cream shops. A few days later, I received a note of apology and four coupons for free ice cream. Biblical principles (God's ways) are real, and they do work! The Bible says, "A fool gives full vent to anger, but a wise person quietly holds it back" (Proverbs 29:11 NLT).

On my way home this past weeknight, eating my first free double chocolate chunk ice-cream cone, I drove past a store that has been closed for several days now. I first noticed that it was closed a few days ago when I drove by during the day. What caught my attention this particular night was that in the dark empty window there was a bright, neon sign that said, "Open." This scene inspired me to wonder how many of us are like this store? We may have a bright smiling "open" sign across our face, and even our talk may sound as if we are open for business, but inside we are dark and empty.

I recently received an e-mail from A Good Word reader who spoke about how on the outside everyone would think that he was a strong Christian, but on the inside he was empty like the empty store. The individual wrote, "On the outside, 'I was a saint' and on the inside, 'I was non-existent'." I share this personal thought because at times we all can get this way. Some of the trials and tests of life that we go through can really beat us down. In our times of weakness, our enemy (Satan) uses the same snare that he has used from the beginning of man's time here on earth, the planting of the seed of doubt. We begin to doubt the Word of God.

You may think, "Robby, I don't ever doubt that the Bible is the Word of God." I say I understand; I don't either. But, I will often find myself in a thought pattern: "Is God really concerned with my day-to-day living? Does He really care about this emptiness that I am feeling?" This seed of doubt sounds just like what can be found in the Book of Genesis, chapter 3: "Now the serpent was more crafty than any of the wild animals the Lord God had made. He said to the woman, 'Did God really say, "You must not eat fruit from any tree in the garden?"" (Genesis 3:1 NIV). The enemy will whisper in our mind, "Did God really say that in all things God works for the good of those who love him? How can He work this out for good?"

Yes, I too get the feeling of emptiness as I get beat down with our day-to-day challenges of life. That's why I look so forward to Sundays! I NEED to go to worship service and get recharged. This is exactly what the Apostle Paul is explaining to us in Romans 12: "Do not conform any longer to the pattern of this world, but be transformed by the renewing of your mind. Then you will be able to test and approve what God's will is–his good, pleasing and perfect will" (Romans 12:2). The ONLY way for us not to get caught up in this world pattern of trials and challenges, to KNOW that God loves us, and to KNOW His good and perfect will for our lives, is to continually renew our minds. We do this by going to church, by reading our Bible, by sharing our faith, and reading Christian encouragements like *A Good Word*.

Now you may be away at school (or very busy in your job) and think, "Robby, I hear you. I believe what you say is true, but I've got so much going on, I just can't seem to work any church or Bible study time in. I desire to walk in God's will, but not just now. I kind of like what I'm doing now. I plan to do it later (tomorrow)."

In my Bible study this week, something caught my attention that I've never picked up on before. After I read it, it really made me ponder it in my heart. The story is about Moses, and Moses has been going before Pharaoh asking for the release of the Israelites. Pharaoh has been refusing, and through Moses, the Lord has been sending terrible plagues to the people of Egypt. One of the plagues was the plague of frogs: "So Aaron stretched out his hand over the waters of Egypt, and the frogs came up and covered the land" (Exodus 8:6). There were frogs everywhere. They were in their houses, in their beds, in their ovens, and on their food preparation tables. It got so bad that Pharaoh sent for Moses and Aaron and said, "Pray to the Lord to take the frogs away from me and my people, and I will let your people go to offer sacrifices to the Lord" (Exodus 8:8). Moses then responded to Pharaoh that he would leave it up to Pharaoh to set a time for Moses to pray to the Lord to remove the frogs. Do you know what Pharaoh's response was?

"Tomorrow, Pharaoh said" (Exodus 8:10). Tomorrow? Tomorrow? Why not NOW?

Sometimes, we say the same thing to the Lord's will, "his good, pleasing and perfect will." We may say, "Lord, I love you and I desire to let You direct my life, but right now, I'm OK. These frogs (sins) do get in my way, and give me challenges. I plan to get rid of them tomorrow and serve you." The danger is, tomorrow may never come. You may get use to frogs being around. The Bible says, "But my people would not listen to me ... So I gave them over to their stubborn hearts to follow their own devices" (Psalms 81:11-12). There is a point of no return for some. You may have an "Open" sign for the world to see, but inside your store is very dark and empty. Be very careful not to go too long ithout sweeping all of the frogs out. A fence may be placed around your heart with a big lock to keep it shut like in the picture above.

Tomorrow? Why not now? The Bibles says, "Do not boast about tomorrow, for you do not know what a day may bring forth" (Proverbs 27:1). Pharaoh's heart was hardened on his "tomorrow". He figured by waiting until tomorrow, something else might happen to his pleasure and he wouldn't have to fully obey the Lord. Hear the Words of God: "See, I am setting before you today a blessing and a curse–the blessing if you obey the commands of the Lord your God that I am giving you today; the curse if you disobey the commands of the Lord your God and turn from the way that I command you today ..." (Deuteronomy 11:26-28).

I encourage you to choose the blessing and obey the commands of our Lord. In the very same manner that I inherited a small blessing (free ice cream) in my story above by obeying biblical principles, you can inherit a much larger blessing, light and a "store" full of purpose. Jesus says, "I have come into the world as a light, so that no one who believes in me should stay in darkness" (John 12:46). Your blessing may be that not only does your "Open" sign shine brightly, but that your "store" is so full of light and purpose that you'll just have to share your abundance with others!

What If?

There is a neat song performed by Nichole Nordeman with the title What If? The words to the song are pretty meaningful when you listen to them carefully. I believe that most of us have asked the same questions that the song asks...

> What if you're right?
> He was just another nice guy.
> What if you're right? What if it's true?
> They say the cross will make a fool of you. What if it's true?
> What if He takes his place in history with all the prophets and the kings?
> Who taught us love and came in peace and then the story ends...
> What then?
>
> But what if you're wrong?
> What if there's more? What if there's hope that
> You've never dreamed of hoping for?

Perhaps at different times in our lives, we get into a trial and we start listening to the conversation in our head that goes on like the first stanza of the song above. We may even say to ourselves, "I thought God was in this? Lord, I thought that I was following your lead and now look at the mess that I'm in. I'm beginning to have my doubts about this whole thing."

I'm sure that Silas was thinking these same thoughts in one of his trials as he traveled with the Apostle Paul. In one of his first trips with Paul, Silas went to the town of Philippi. In that town, shortly after their arrival, a young slave girl met up with them. She had the ability to tell the future and, "She earned a great deal of money for her owners by fortune-telling" (Acts 16:16 NIV).

This slave girl followed Paul and Silas around shouting: "These men are servants of the Most High God, who are telling you the way to be saved" (Acts 16:17). The Bible says that she continued to do this for many days. Now Silas may have been thinking that this is pretty neat. God must really be in this for him. Here he is in this foreign city, on his first trip as a missionary for the Lord, and as they walk around they have this local celebrity fortuneteller shouting out their purpose for being there.

On the other hand, this slave girl was annoying Paul. He didn't need any help from this girl that the Bible says, "had a spirit" (Acts 16:16). This was an evil spirit. After getting so annoyed by the girl the Bible says, "Finally Paul became so troubled that he turned around and said to the spirit, 'In the name of Jesus Christ I command you to come out of her!' At that moment the spirit left her."

If I were Silas, right now I would be thinking that I'm right where God wanted me to be. God's hand is all over this. I am following His lead and I'm seeing miracles and receiving the blessings of following and believing. I would be pretty "puffed up" at this point, but look what happens next. The Bible tells us in Acts 16:19, "When the owners of the slave girl realized that their hope of making money was gone, they seized Paul and Silas and dragged them into the marketplace to face the authorities." The story goes on to say, "The crowd joined in the attack against Paul and Silas, and the magistrates ordered them to be stripped and beaten. After they had been severely flogged, they were thrown into prison, and the jailer was commanded to guard them carefully. Upon receiving such orders, he put them in the inner cell and fastened their feet in the stocks" (Acts 16:22-24).

Boy what a turn-around! As Silas, one moment everything seems to be wonderful with God's blessings all over it; the next minute the bottom falls out. You feel as if you've been exposed publicly, beaten down, and thrown into the deepest hole all bound up. Has anything like this ever happened to you? Have you ever been thinking that you were living God's will for your life and suddenly the bottom seems to fall out from beneath you? You may have been thrown head first into an unexpected trial?

In the story, if I'm Silas I'm thinking, "Wow, what just happened to me? I thought that I was walking with the Lord's blessings? How can this happen to me? A loving God wouldn't have allowed this to happen to me?" What becomes worse in moments like this, the enemy (Satan and his demons) gets into full court pressure to attack. His methods have never changed since Genesis. He begins to get you to question the things that you knew were true. In the Book of Genesis he says to Eve, "Did God really say, 'You must not eat from any tree in the garden?'" (Genesis 3:1). In the Book of Matthew 4:2, while Jesus was in one of His first trials fasting in the desert for forty days the Bible says, "he was hungry." When Jesus was down, then Satan came and tried to get Jesus to question the things that He knew were true. Satan continued to say, "If you are the son of God …"

When you are in a trial, don't believe the lies that "just pop" into your head. You may even begin to ask the same questions as the first stanza to the song above. Just have the faith to start singing the second stanza! There is more! There is more hope than you've ever dreamed before! When you start singing praises to God, great things begin to happen. The Bible says, "And we know that in all things God works for the good of those who love him …" (Romans 8:28).

You may ask, "So Robby, what good did God work out in the story above for Silas?" I'm glad that you asked … Do you know what the Bible says that Silas did in this moment of his deepest trial? He started singing praises to the Lord, "About midnight Paul and Silas were praying and singing hymns to God, and the other prisoners were listening to them" (Acts 16:25). You say, "OK Robby, I get the praise singing part, but how does God work this out for His good?" Keep reading: "Suddenly there was such a violent earthquake that the foundations of the prison were shaken. At once all the prison doors flew open, and everybody's chains came loose" (Acts 16:26). The story goes on to say that the jailer thought that he had lost the prisoners that he had been assigned to keep. He was about to kill himself over the loss but then Paul called out to him that they were still there. The Bible says, "The jailer called for lights, rushed in and fell trembling before Paul and Silas. He then brought them out and asked, "Sirs, what must I do to be saved?" (v. 30). The story goes on to say that the jailer and his whole family came to believe in Jesus that very night.

I want to encourage you to keep the faith when you're thrown into a trial. It's understandable for a moment to think about the first stanza to the song above, but cast those thoughts out quickly and believe in the hope that you have in the Lord. The Bible says, "No, in all these things, (these things meaning the trials we go through), we are more than conquerors through him who loved us" (Romans 8:37). That is A Good Word! Others around you will see your faith shining through in your difficult moment. You will never know how many "jailer's families" your faith will impact in a positive way for the Lord. Amen.

You're Not Good Enough

Just in case you don't recognize the picture above, it is a picture of Simon Cowell's trademark. Simon is one of the celebrity judges on the popular TV show "American Idol." Yes, I do watch the show, and yes, I know that Simon is not very supportive of Christian songs performed on the show. I hope that you were able to catch the show the season when Dolly Parton appeared as a special guest. She performed a Christian song about Jesus, and then made a special remark to Simon following the song.

Simon has actually helped to make this show to be the most watched show on TV today. He does this by expressing frank remarks of his opinion about the singing performance of the contestant after each song. Many times his comment is just plain mean. He will often tell a contestant that, "You're not good enough to be a singer. Find a new job."

As mean as I do think a comment like this is in front of the contestant on national TV, I do, however, believe that there is some merit to his honesty. Now if I were a judge on this show I would be more like Paula Abdul. She only says nice things. After a bad performance she might say, "Oh, you look so beautiful tonight. You just make me smile each time that I see you perform. No matter what, you will always be a champion in my heart." She probably was raised like I was. My mom taught me to follow the teachings of Thumper's father in the classic cartoon movie *Bambi*. Thumper looks at a young Bambi and says,

> Thumper: "He doesn't walk very good, does he?
> Thumper's Mom: "Thumper!"
> Thumper: "Yes, mama?"
> Thumper's Mom: "What did your father tell you this morning?"
> Thumper: {clears throat} "If you can't say something nice— don't say nothing at all."

I love Paula, but I really don't care about what she has to say to each performer, because I know that she is going to only say something nice. Now there is nothing wrong about being nice, but sometimes inserting honesty as well may be better. If you watch the show, you will know that the contestants desire Simon's affirmation the most. There is a desire in all of us that wants to hear the truth. Do you know where you can find truth?

My family and home were recently selected as a place to film a pilot for a reality TV show. A contestant performed for our entire family in our home. We were supposed to give our real opinions of this person's performance. (The contestant actually was not very good, and doesn't need to pursue a career in this endeavor at this time.) But, I would not let my family give a real opinion answer in front of the camera in view of the contestant. I told my family, "We don't want to hurt her feelings, so say something nice." Several days later I heard my daughter telling someone else about how bad the performance of the contestant was. I thought to myself that perhaps some honesty might have benefited the person in the long run.

That being said, I'm going to be honest with you and say to you the same thing as the title to my lesson above, "You're not good enough." Now that I've hurt your feelings, please don't close this book to look for affirmation from another book. The truth of the matter is— I'm not good enough either. There's that word "truth" again. There was a Roman governor many years ago named Pilot. Pilot asked Jesus, "What is truth?" Jesus had just told Pilot the answer. He said, "I came into the world, to testify to the truth. Everyone on the side of truth listens to me" (John 18:37-38).

Several years ago I was visiting with my older sister, Sherryl. I was in my early stage of seeking the Lord and His possible purpose for my life. Normally in my earlier years I wouldn't discuss religion at all. I had my personal thoughts of religion and everyone else had their personal thoughts. I didn't want to share mine, and I didn't want to hear other's share theirs with me. But at my sister's house, I was in a new chapter of my life, seeking to draw nearer to the Lord. I was finally excited to share with her some of the ways that I felt that the Lord was calling me. In our conversation she asked me, "How do you know that you are going to heaven?" I'm not sure if I had ever been personally asked this question before. I ask you to pause and think to yourself what your answer would be right now to this question. (Pause for a moment, what is your answer?)

I began my answer, "Well, I'm a good person. I care about the poor, I cry in sad movie scenes, I give to charities, I'm kind to people, I'm a good father to my children ..." I'm sure that I said many more things that I did to justify my entry ticket to heaven. My sister then answered, "All of those things are good, but you're not good enough." Talk about taking the wind out of my sail. Here I was on a roll, all puffed up and telling her how wonderful God must view me, and she tells me that I'm not good enough! "Well, I've never ..."

The Bible says, "The Lord looks down from heaven on the sons of men to see if there are any who understand, any who seek God. All have turned aside, they have together become corrupt; there is no one who does good, not even one" (Psalm 14:2-3 and Romans 3:10-12 NIV). Now you may ask, "Robby, when I give to a Christian charity, isn't that good? What could the Bible possibly mean by, "there is no one who does good?" My answer is, yes that is good that you give to a Christian charity, but in all that good meaning, it will not earn you a ticket into heaven. I heard that a very famous millionaire of Atlanta fame once said that he may not be sitting on the fifty-yard line in heaven, but he will be in the upper deck because he gave so much of his money to charity. Do you think this will get him into heaven?

For this lesson I will list two views of good that we do: the way that man views good, and the ways that God views good. For the ways that man views as good, I could write pages and pages of good works. For the way that God views as good, He gave us His measuring stick through Moses. You can find the measurement device in Exodus 20:1-17. It is called the Ten Commandments. Back in my conversation with my sister, I mentioned how I felt that God must very proud of me, and all the nice things that I did. The Bible says, "for all have sinned and fall short of the glory of God ..." (Romans 3:23). Even though I did many good deeds, my works fell short of God's glory. By God's measuring stick, the Ten Commandments (the law), I fell way short of pleasing Him. The Bible says, "Therefore no one will be declared righteous in his sight by observing the law..." (Romans 3:20). So, if God is viewing me by the Ten Commandments, I'm not doing very well. The Bible says, "For whoever keeps the whole law and yet stumbles at just one point is guilty of breaking all of it" (James 2:10). You may be thinking, "Boy, Robby, I come here for a little good news and now I don't feel so good. It's impossible to keep from breaking the Ten Commandments, and now you tell me if I break just one–one time, I've broken all of them?" I say yes that is correct, but keep reading. I do have good news for you!

I have heard some people say, "My god is a loving god. He just wouldn't allow me to go to a place of eternal torment and fire: "the fiery furnace, where there will be weeping and gnashing of teeth" (Matthew 13:42). They go on to say: "At the judgment seat I would tell god all the good things that I did for him. I would convince him that my good outweighed my bad." I say, two things: First–be very careful about breaking the second commandment here, "You shall have no other gods before me" (Exodus 20:3). This made-up god and the God of the Bible are not the same. Secondly: the Bible says, "Now we know that whatever the law says, it says to those who are under the law, so that every mouth may be silenced and the whole world held accountable to God" (Romans 3:19). Standing before a Holy God at the judgment seat, if you are being judged by the law, you just won't be able to speak. (See Matthew 22:12.)

Several years ago, I received my first traffic ticket. I was charged with running through a red light. I can remember very well the place and the circumstances. It was raining cats-and-dogs and I was driving very slowly. As I approached the traffic light, I saw it turn red just as I was underneath it. (Remember, I was driving about 20 miles per hour.) Well, since I moved through the intersection so slowly, the traffic cop perceived to think that I ran the light on purpose. (I now do what all other Atlanta drivers do on a yellow light–gun it!) I received a court date to go before the judge. For weeks I planned in my mind how I would explain to the judge that I was not guilty. I would tell him what a good driver I was. I would tell him that I followed all traffic laws, and I never had been charged before. I went to my court date. It was a huge room, full of people everywhere. One after another would go before the judge and tell him their excuses and reasons. No one claimed to be guilty. Then came my turn. I had practiced over and over in my head what I would say when I got before the judge. I was called to the front. Standing in front of hundreds of people, with the judge looking down on me, he read my charge. My heart was pounding out of my chest; I could barely stand straight. He asked, "How do you plea?" With all the energy that I could muster up, I opened my mouth and all I could say was, "Guilty." Boom was the sound of the gavel, and over to the clerk I went to pay my fine. Being judged by the law will be much more nerve racking than this.

Now for the good news: The word "gospel" comes from the Latin translation of good tale, or good news. I will share the gospel truth. You don't have to be judged by the law. Jesus gives us the truth in John 14:6: "I am the way and the truth." Jesus tells us in John 3:16, "For God so loved the world that he gave his one and only Son, that whoever believes in him shall not perish but have eternal life." You might ask, "Robby, I've heard this before. But what does it mean that God gave His one and Only Son?" The answer is found in 2 Corinthians 5:21: "God made him who had no sin to be sin for us, so that in him we might become the righteousness of God." Jesus paid our fine to the Judge. We are no longer under the law if we place our hope and trust in Jesus as our Savior. The Bible says, "Christ redeemed us from the curse of the law by becoming a curse for us …" (Galatians 3:13). He paid our fine on the cross.

The old Gospel song says that Jesus paid it all. In my earlier story about me going before the judge, I would have loved for someone to go up to the judge and say, "Judge, I'm paying Robby's fine. Charge his crime to my record. Robby has placed his trust in me to represent himself before you." In this manner, I would not have had to be judged by the law. Jesus makes this offer to you if you will place your trust in Him. He will stand before God and say, "This one is mine. I paid his fine." "For Christ has entered into heaven itself to appear now before God as our Advocate" (Hebrews 9:24 NLT). He will be your Advocate, "if you confess with your mouth, 'Jesus is Lord,' and believe in your heart that God raised him from the dead, you will be saved" (Romans 10:9).

The song goes: And when before Thy throne
I stand in Him complete
Jesus died my soul to save
My lips shall still repeat

Jesus paid it all
All to Him I owe
Sin hath left a crimson stain
He washed it white as snow

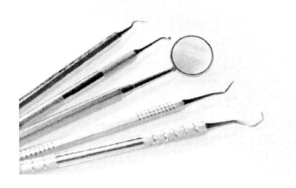

Going to the Dentist

In one of my lessons, called "Your True Value" (in this book), I speak of a visit to the True Value Hardware store. It was a visit to the store that inspired a lesson. My great friend and spiritual encourager, Mark Keel, joked with me after the posting of the lesson. He said, "That was a good word! I can't wait until you visit Big Lots and write a lesson about the title of that store."

It's neat the way that I am inspired to write. Most of my lessons are about topics that someone has mentioned or something that I have picked up by personal observation during the week. The lesson today came to my mind the other morning while I was in the shower. I was getting ready for the new day, but not looking forward to my first task. You see, I had an appointment with the dentist. I was dreading it.

As a kid, going to the dentist was a breeze. I would have my teeth cleaned, and the dentist would walk in for about two minutes and look into my mouth. He'd normally say, "All looks good, see you again in six months." No big deal, right? Well, with getting older, things change a little. As our bodies get older, things change. Our teeth can easily begin to get small cracks in them. This is the result of regular chewing over the years. The way to fix the cracks is to get a crown made for your tooth.

I was dreading the dentist visit because I have one of these cracks in a tooth. I was scheduled for a regular visit, but I knew that the dentist was going to remind me again that I needed to schedule a visit to crown that tooth before it gets worse. I didn't want to go because I didn't want to hear what I already knew was bad news. "Perhaps if I cancelled the visit," I thought to myself, "I wouldn't have to think about that crown again until a few months later. I wouldn't be bothered by news of a change I needed to make that would, in the long run, make my life better."

You may be saying now, "Robby, where are you going with this?" Let me explain. At that moment in the shower, a thought came to me, "You know Robby, that's how many people think about going to church." We know that we should go to church. The Bible tells us in Jeremiah 31:33 that God placed His ways, His laws, in our heart. God says, "I will put my law in their minds and write it on their hearts." The Apostle Paul writes to us, in Romans 2: 14-16, that the ways and laws of God are written on our hearts. In this passage, He says that we know when our own thoughts are bad: "since they show that the requirements of the law are written on their hearts, their consciences also bearing witness, and their thoughts now accusing ..." Paul was writing about the Gentiles (us), which is everyone who is not a Jew.

Inside, we really know that there is God. Many try to push the thought out by trying to use logic and worldly reasoning. These folks won't get it until they turn their thoughts to their inner spirit. The Bible tells us in 1 Corinthians 2: 10-11: "God has revealed it to us by his Spirit. The Spirit searches all things, even the deep things of God. For who among men knows the thoughts of a man except the man's spirit within him?"

I have received e-mails and have talked to many people that say that they don't like "a fear based religion." They will go on to say that they don't like to attend church because the Pastor will say something that will try to "scare" them into believing or doing what is right. They often believe that a "loving god" wouldn't want them to feel bad or be scared to live the way that they are living. I heard about a very famous male actor who has become a member of the Church of Scientology. I was told that he made the statement that he liked his religion much better than the other because it doesn't have all the strict rules to follow. What does your true inner Spirit think about this?

I'm here today to encourage you by telling you that God does love you. He wants to bless you. That is exactly why He uses preachers, Sunday school teachers, and others (like me) to tell you the truth. God does have laws and strict rules for us to follow. This is what The Bible teaches us. This is why there are old stories in the Old Testament that gives us great insight on how we should be living today. In the Book of Jeremiah, chapter 36, the Lord told Jeremiah to write down on a scroll the words that He was about to speak. God wanted there to be no misunderstanding by the people. He wanted them to know that He was disappointed by their sinful ways and if they didn't change soon, disaster was on its way.

God said in Jeremiah 36:3, "Perhaps when the people of Judah hear about every disaster I plan to inflict on them, each of them will turn from his wicked way; then I will forgive their wickedness and their sin." This one verse tells us a great deal about God's way. When He used the word "perhaps," this implies that the people needed to respond to His warning. Then He goes on to say, "each one of them." This tells us that it is not a group thing that He is looking for. He wants us as individuals to make a choice. I tell my children often, "Life is full of choices." Each day you have choices to make. Is your selection of choice for God's glory, or is it to satisfy a "worldly" desire? God goes on to tell us in the passage above that if we turn from our sinful ways, He will forgive us. But, if we choose to go against God's ways, He will allow us. Disaster will come. Believe me! OOPS–There I go using scare tactics.

No. I love you too. I want you to walk in God's favor. I want you to receive all the blessings that God has in store for you. I don't want the consequences of sin to show up in your life. We all need to encourage each other to stay in the race: "let us throw off everything that hinders and the sin that so easily entangles, and let us run with perseverance the race marked out for us" (Hebrews 12:1).

My dentist is trying to help me by telling me what I don't want to hear. Even though it may be a little painful, I need to hear it and heed his advice. If I go on ignoring it, the problem will not go away, and I WILL suffer a disaster. I could be out of state and a long way from my dentist if/when my tooth breaks. An exposed nerve would be MUCH more painful than a little time in his chair to fix the crack now.

Is the same possible for you if you don't heed the advice of your pastor or Christian counselor? Could your small crack in your walk with the Lord become a complete break that will cause disaster and pain?

Go to church, pray, listen to what God is telling you. "For I know the plans I have for you," declares the Lord, "plans to prosper you and not to harm you, plans to give you hope and a future"–God– (Jeremiah 29:11).

He Is Not Here

S everal years ago I grew up quickly in one year. I married my college sweetheart, graduated from college, started my first job, and had my first child (Joshua) pretty much all within a year's time. During that time I worked an extra one day per week as a church custodian cleaning a church and Sunday school rooms in preparation of the Sunday events. You probably think, "Robby that is so neat, you served the Lord even way back then." Well no. I needed the extra money, so I spent several hours in the church each Saturday just cleaning. It wasn't so bad if I would make myself get up early on Saturday morning and go ahead and knock it out before lunch. But on the days that I was lazy, I paid the price of being in a very large dark building all by myself. This was during a time in my life when Jesus was missing. Perhaps I would find Him in the church one day?

I can remember very well the Saturdays that I decided to start my cleaning job late in the afternoon. I suppose a ballgame or something would be on TV that I didn't want to miss earlier in the day, therefore I would just go late. It was during these dark nights alone in the church that I was fearful that the Lord would just show up behind me while I had the vacuum cleaner running loud. You see, I knew that I was in His house; therefore, I would never cut corners in my work. (During that time I figured that He was watching me, and would be very disappointed if I failed to vacuum one room before Sunday.) But my biggest fear was that He would show up behind me and say, "Robby." I had heard about the Lord's "calling" of people, and I thought if I were to be "called", He would do it in that dark church when I was all alone since He lived here— or did He? No, he is not here, but where is He?

One of the earliest signs of the Lord's presence, the Shechinah glory of God, is found in the Book of Exodus as the way He guided the Hebrew people out of Egypt: "By day the Lord went ahead of them in a pillar of cloud to guide them on their way ..." (Exodus 13:21 NIV). Later in the same Book, when Moses followed God's instructions to build the first Tent of Meeting, the tabernacle, God's presence shows up to dwell: "Then the cloud covered the Tent of Meeting, and the glory of the Lord filled the tabernacle. Moses could not enter the Tent of Meeting because the cloud had settled upon it, and the glory of the Lord filled the tabernacle" (Exodus 40:34).

Almost five-hundred years later, King Solomon followed God's instructions to build a permanent tabernacle, later called Solomon's Temple. When the temple was finished, King Solomon summoned for the Ark of the Covenant and it was placed in the: "inner sanctuary of the temple, the Most Holy Place, and put it beneath the wings of the cherubim" (1 Kings 8:6). The Bible says, "When the priests withdrew from the Holy Place, the cloud filled the temple of the Lord. And the priests could not perform their service because of the cloud, for the glory of the Lord filled his temple" (1 Kings 8:10-11).

You may ask, "So Robby, you're telling me that the Lord actually did reside (dwell) in the church, (the temple), at one time?" My answer is that God's presence was certainly there as noted above, and Solomon did say, "The Lord has said that he would dwell in a dark cloud; I have indeed built a magnificent temple for you, a place for you to dwell forever" (1 Kings 8:12-13). But Solomon will answer this question best in his prayer of dedication of the temple to the Lord: "But will God really dwell on earth? The heavens, even the highest heaven, cannot contain you. How much less this temple I have built!" (1 Kings 8:27). So, if you go searching for Him in Solomon's Temple, He is not here.

God's chosen people, the Hebrews, turned from God, and God allowed the Babylonians to conquer Jerusalem and destroy the temple: "On the seventh day of the fifth month, in the nineteenth year of

Nebuchadnezzar king of Babylon, Nebuzaradan commander of the imperial guard, an official of the king of Babylon, came to Jerusalem. He set fire to the temple of the Lord, the royal palace and all the houses of Jerusalem. Every important building he burned down" (2 Kings 25: 8-9). The presence of God was gone and not to be found for many years. So, if you searched through the burned ashes trying to find Him, He is not here.

Several years later: "In the second year of King Darius, on the first day of the sixth month, the word of the Lord came through the prophet Haggai to Zerubbabel ..." (Haggai 1:1). This very short two chapter Book has become one of my favorites. I could actually write several lessons from this two page, two-chapter Book of the Bible. I will share some very neat things about this chapter. First, the Lord was ready for His house to be built again: "This is what the Lord Almighty says: 'These people say, "The time has not come for the Lord's house to be built." 'Then the word of the Lord came through the prophet Haggai: 'Is it a time for yourselves to be living in your paneled houses, while this house remains a ruin?'" (Haggai 1:2-4). So Zerubbabel takes the task on to rebuild the temple. The temple comes to be known as the second temple, or Zerubbabel's Temple. God is pleased by Zerubbabel and says to him," 'I will make you like my signet ring, for I have chosen you', declares the Lord Almighty" (Haggai 2:23). Another neat thing about this chapter is that Zerubbabel is one of the first descendants of King David in a long time that God was pleased with. Look where Zerubbabel's heritage ends up: Turn to Matthew 1:13 and look at the genealogy of Jesus through Joseph. Now turn to Luke 3:27 and follow the genealogy of Jesus through Mary's family tree. Zerubbabel is the only man beneath King David in each genealogy that leads to the birth of Jesus.

So Zerrubbabel builds the temple and the Lord says," 'The glory of this present house will be greater than the glory of the former house,' says the Lord Almighty" (Haggai 2:9). I ask you to consider two things about this chapter: First, it must be important to the Lord that we have a community place of worship for Him. Does He really need a house in which to dwell? He likes for us to gather as a community of believers to give Him worship. The Book of Hebrews says, "Let us not give up meeting together, as some are in the habit of doing, but let us encourage one another–and all the more as you see the Day approaching" (Hebrews

10:25). The second thing for you to consider is this: what do you think that God meant by His words, "The glory of this present house will be greater than the glory of the former house … "? I ask, how can His glory be greater in this new temple? (It was much smaller.) In Solomon's temple His glory showed as in a dark cloud. Some of the older Jewish people remembered the glory of the old temple and missed that glory, but no cloud appeared in the new. He is not here.

Some 500 years later the glory did show up in that temple, and the Glory dwelled among the people: "The Word became flesh and made his dwelling among us. We have seen his glory, the glory of the One and Only, who came from the father, full of grace and truth" (John 1:14). The glory of the present house became greater than the former: "When he was twelve years old, they went up to the Feast, according to custom. After the Feast was over, while his parents were returning home, the boy Jesus stayed behind in Jerusalem … After three days they found him in the temple courts, sitting among the teachers … 'Why were you searching for me?' he asked. "Didn't you know I had to be in my father's house?" (Luke 2:42-49). The Bible says, "Then he went down to Nazareth with them and was obedient to them" (Luke 2:51). The Greater Glory had returned to the temple, but then He left with his parents … He is not here.

The Greater Glory came not to live in the temple, but: "For God so loved the world that he gave his one and only Son, that whoever believes in him shall not perish but have eternal life. For God did not send his Son into the world to condemn the world, but save the world through him. Whoever believes in him is not condemned, but whoever does not believe stands condemned already because he has not believed in the name of God's one and only Son" (John 3:16-18). Jesus came into this world not to condemn us for our sinful nature, but to save us from an eternal separation from God (hell). For, "If we confess our sins, he is faithful and just and will forgive us our sin and purify us from unrighteousness" (1 John 1:9). Jesus gave Himself to die on the cross as: "the atoning sacrifice for our sins, and not only for ours but also for the sins of the whole world" (1 John 2:2). Now you may ask, "So Robby, if I want to find Jesus I look to the cross?" No, they removed Him from the cross and placed Him in a tomb. So if you look for Him on the cross, He is not here.

Are you looking for Jesus? Is He missing in your life? I just told you where they placed Him. The Bible says that a man named Joseph from Arimathea asked for the body of Jesus, "Then he took it down, wrapped it in linen cloth and placed it in a tomb cut in the rock, one which no one had yet been laid" (Luke 23: 53). Perhaps you are like I was just a few years ago. I knew who Jesus was, but He was missing in my life. I had heard that some people had found Him, but I didn't really know what that meant. Maybe they looked for Him in the tomb. Can we find Him there?

> After the Sabbath, at dawn on the first day of the week, (Sunday) Mary Magdalene and the other Mary went to look at the tomb. There was a violent earthquake, for an angel of the Lord came down from heaven and, going to the tomb, rolled back the stone and sat on it. His appearance was like lightning, and his clothes were white as snow. The guards were so afraid of him that they shook and became like dead men. The angel said to the women, 'Do not be afraid, for I know that you are looking for Jesus, who was crucified. He is not here; he has risen … (Matthew 28:1-6).

Perhaps this angel is speaking to you here? He says, "for I know that you are looking for Jesus …" I've covered many places where He is not in this lesson. I can help you find Him by seeking Him in the same place that I found Him. The neat thing about it is, you can find Him right now, wherever you are and whatever you are doing! The Bible says that He is very near to you: "The word is near you; it is in your mouth and in your heart, that is the word of faith we are proclaiming: That if you confess with your mouth, 'Jesus is Lord,' and believe in your heart that God raised him from the dead, you will be saved" (Romans 10:8-9).

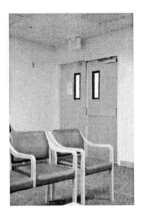

Your Frequent Illnesses

I spent some time in a waiting room very much like the picture above this week. I am certain that you have some experience doing this same thing. My time this week was spent in the waiting area of the Women's Breast Care Specialist of Atlanta, Georgia as I waited for my wife Julie to be examined. I knew in advance that the wait would be a while, so I was prepared with a new book and my ipod music device. I never read any of my book.

We arrived very early, and Julie was called away very soon after our arrival which left me alone in the lobby. As I sat there, patient after patient began to come in and fill the room. Many women also came with their husbands, but most of them were all alone. I would watch each patient come to the front desk to sign in with the receptionist. Most would smile, but I could tell that it was more of a nervous smile as they received the forms to fill out.

As I witnessed the concern on each patient's face, my heart began to be exposed to the worry that each was going through. I began to pray for each lady that stepped up to the counter. I would say, "Lord, bless this lady. Please heal any disease or illness that she may have." I started thinking about the love and concern that I had for my wife, and I knew that each woman had someone with the same thoughts about them. At this time, the guy sitting next to me must of thought that I was reading a very sad book because to hide my tears, I opened my book and looked down to its pages. I noticed his glances at me as I kept wiping my eyes. I'm sure this guy was thinking, "Why would this man be crying while he reads a book about basketball coach Rick Pitino?"

My thoughts were, "Lord, I wish I had the power of healing. I would just touch each woman as they walked in and them send them home in Your name." But the Lord does not work this way. I would love to believe the "healings" that I see on TV, but I'm very concerned that these guys will be held accountable one day for their demonstrations. They need to be walking up and down the hospital corridors instead of "performing" on large stages.

So as I sat in the waiting area seeing so many patients come in, I asked the same questions that you may ask at times: If God is in control, why does He allow illness, disease, and even death? He especially should prevent believers from disease, shouldn't He? Some people actually believe that a Christian with faith can't get cancer or any disease. They will quote from the Book of Isaiah 53:5, "But he was pierced for our transgressions, he was crushed for our iniquities; the punishment that brought us peace was upon him, and by his wounds we are healed" (NIV). That is a wonderful verse, but it doesn't say that we are healed from all illnesses and diseases. (We are healed from the eternal separation from God by believing upon Jesus as our Savior.)

I do believe in the healing power of prayer. I have personally witnessed this blessing. But I have also personally witnessed what seem to be unanswered prayers for healing. I have many great Christian friends, who have serious illnesses, and I have prayed for their healing, but they have continued to be plagued by illness. Why would God choose to heal some, but not others? Why did Jesus, with all of the healing power that He had, not go around and heal every person that He came near? It has always been a question in my mind about the pool of Bethesda found in John chapter 5. The Bible says, "Here a great number of disabled people used to lie - the blind, the lame, the paralyzed. One who was there had been invalid for thirty-eight years. When Jesus saw him lying there and learned that he had been in this condition for a long time, he asked him, "Do you want to get well?" (John 5:3-6 NIV). Now, if you wanted to start your own cult by taking one scripture from the

Bible and twisting the meaning, you could start the "you must be sick 38 years before healing" cult. But I wonder why Jesus just didn't heal everyone around the pool? Wouldn't that really catch the attention of all people of Jerusalem? Why just "One"? The only answer for this is found in Isaiah 55:8, "For my thoughts are not your thoughts, neither are your ways my ways,' declares the Lord." We will just never know the answer to many questions like this on this side of heaven.

Wouldn't it be nice if when we became Christians, we never had to experience illness or disease? Why wouldn't a loving God make it be this way? Wouldn't everyone want to become a believer then? Surely much more of the world would believe in Jesus then. Or would the world really believe? Perhaps people would want its benefits, but not the submission.

You may be thinking, "OK Robby, you've asked enough questions. I've thought about these same questions. But where is the encouragement here? I've had to deal with illness and disease personally. How does this fit into the promise found in Jeremiah 29? ("For I know the plans I have for you...plans to prosper you and not to harm you, plans to give you a hope and a future.") Sometimes my own personal faith is challenged by my questions." I say I understand.

As I study the Bible each week, different scriptures that I read and hear seem to stand out more than before. This week, the scripture found in Paul's letter to Timothy, stood out stronger than before. The Books of 1 Timothy, and 2 Timothy are letters from the Apostle Paul to Timothy, who worked as an emissary of Paul to nurture new Christian churches. Timothy was like a Pastor to new beginning churches. Let me first say that the Lord used Paul to heal a crippled man, "who had been lame from birth and never walked," in Lystra. (Acts 14:8-10) So here we have a wonderful man of God, Paul, who wrote most of our New Testament, writing a letter to a young new preacher Timothy. Paul writes, "Stop drinking only water, and use a little wine because of your stomach and your frequent illnesses" (1 Timothy 5:23). Did you catch that? Apparently, Timothy had frequent illnesses. Paul loved Timothy very much. Why wouldn't a man who healed a cripple man just call Timothy over, lay hands on him, and heal him from all of his illnesses? Do you question the faith of Paul or Timothy? I sure don't. Our Lord used Timothy in many wonderful ways, even though he was often ill. Perhaps his illness brought him before people that he wouldn't have normally met. Can God work this way? ABOSOLUTELY!

Turn to the Book of Galatians. The Book starts, "Paul, an apostle-sent not from men nor by man, but by Jesus Christ and God the Father..." (Galatians 1:1). Who sent Paul to Galatia? He just said the answer - sent "but by Jesus Christ." How did our Lord send him? Paul tells us in Galatians 4:13, "As you know, it was because of an illness that I first preached the gospel to you." What? It was an illness that brought Paul to preach to the people of Galatia? Whose illness was it? Was Timothy sick again? Let's keep reading... Paul says in the next verse, "Even though my illness was a trial to you, you did not treat me with contempt or scorn. Instead, you welcomed me as if I were an angel of God, as if I were Christ Jesus himself"(vs.14). I can understand why God would allow one of His most beloved followers to become ill now. Paul went through many hardships, but I know where Paul prospered and where his future filled with hope ended. Perhaps you can understand Paul better now as he writes, "Be joyful in hope, patient in affliction, faithful in prayer. Share with God's people who are in need" (Romans 12:12-13).

I am very concerned with the illness of the women I saw this week. I am very concerned about any illness that you or your family may be going through. Paul tells us, "Be joyful always; pray continually; give thanks in all circumstances, for this is God's will for you in Christ Jesus" (1 Thessalonians 5:16-18). How can this illness (affliction) be for any good? The Psalmist in Psalms 119:71 says, "It was good for me to be afflicted so that I might learn your decrees." Pray that the Lord uses this time to draw you nearer to Him. I pray for your healing!

Though That Was Shorter

As I was reading from the Old Testament this week, the four words in the title stood out to me. Can you guess where these four are found?

After I read these words in the scripture, I thought to myself, "If God is God, why would He do this? The Creator of this world certainly has the power to prevent the need." (Why doesn't He allow us the easiest route in our journey of day-to-day living?) This passage in my Bible (I will cover it below) caused me to dwell on those four words for a few days. I came to realize the answer to my question, and more importantly, I found answers to many questions about why God won't do something (on our timetable).

This past week I heard that a young new believer made the comment that God doesn't listen to his prayers. It seems the answer to the prayers were not provided fast enough, therefore doubt set in. Do you ever wonder why your requests to God seem to go unanswered? Perhaps you are even "armed" for the short and fast answers by doing all of the proper "stuff" like reading your Bible, going to church, praying, and trying to be a better person, but you seem to be wandering on your own as if you were in a dry desert.

In the Book of Exodus, the Bible tells the great story of Moses and the chosen people of God, the Israelites. Moses had gone before

Pharaoh several times to ask that the Israelites be released from their bondage of slavery. As the result of several plagues cast upon Pharaoh and his people, Pharaoh finally gave in (the Lord unhardened Pharaoh's heart) and let the people of God go. This happened just after the Bible says, "At midnight the Lord struck down all the firstborn in Egypt, from the firstborn of Pharaoh, who sat on the throne, to the firstborn of the prisoner, who was in the dungeon, and the firstborn of all the livestock as well" (Exodus 12:29 NIV). The Israelites didn't lift a finger in a battle, and the Lord struck down thousands.

The Bible says, "When Pharaoh let the people go, God did not lead them on the road through the Philistine country, **though that was shorter**" (Exodus 13:17). What? Why did God not lead His chosen people to the Promised Land by the shorter road? If you look at a map, you will notice that the shortest route to today's Israel from Egypt would be by following the coast of the "Great Sea" (the Mediterranean) through the land of the Philistines (the current Gaza Strip). This would have taken only days to reach the Promised Land instead of the forty years that it ended up taking.

The Bible goes on to say why God did not send the Israelites up the shorter path, "For God said, 'If they face war, they might change their minds and return to Egypt.' So God led the people around by the desert road toward the Red Sea. The Israelites went up out of Egypt armed for battle" (Exodus 13:17-18). This is very interesting to me. The Bible tells us that the people were armed for battle, but God did not want them to face a battle so early on. Back to the beginning of my lesson: I asked why wouldn't our omnipotent God who just killed thousands of Egyptians (without the help of any battle), send the Israelites right up the Mediterranean through the land of the Philistines and wipe out any foe that gets in the way? He is God, right?

So I ask, "Why does God sometimes send us around the long path that may seem to be like we are walking through a dry desert, instead of answering our prayers for a quick fix? He is God, isn't He? He could just heal, repair, change, fix our situation immediately if He desired, couldn't He? The Bible tells us in Isaiah 55:8, "For my thoughts are not your thoughts, neither are your ways my ways." This scripture is not very comforting to us when we are hurting, and we desire an answer to our prayers right away to heal our hurt. But then I think to myself, "Would I want God to answer prayers for my ways, or would I rather wait and be in His will for His ways?" As difficult as it is sometimes, I've learned to wait on His ways. Oh, I want to go out and try to fix some of my problems and trials in a fast way. I will even be tempted to send up a short prayer and say, "Lord, if you don't want me to do such and so to fix this, please close the door." But, in the end, I just turn it over to Him and say, "I need a little help here, Lord. I'm giving it to You to handle from here." Jesus taught us to pray in what we call the Lord's Prayer, "your will be done on earth as it is in heaven" (Matthew 6:10). God's will is the best for us.

Looking back, my path of spiritual growth has taken me down the long route toward the Red Sea. I wondered many times why in the world would the Israelites turn away from God and build a golden calf after they personally witnessed the parting of the Red Sea to escape Pharaoh and his army? But now I understand. Very early in my new walk, I witnessed a great work that could have only come from the Lord. I knew it was God, but I was still holding on to part of Egypt (slavery to sin). Even though I began to share my faith, read my Bible, and attend church each week, I still looked back and visited Egypt ever so often. So I continued my journey around the long path. Sometimes, we just aren't ready for the short path.

Jesus taught a parable: "A farmer went out to sow his seed. As he was scattering the seed, some fell along the path, and the birds came and ate it up. Some fell on rocky places, where it did not have much soil. It sprang up quickly, because the soil was shallow. But when the sun came up, the plants were scorched, and they withered because they had no root" (Matthew 13:3-6). How deep is your root? Are you spending time with the Lord, developing a deeper understanding, rooted in the Word of God? The Bible says, "But blessed is the man who trusts in the Lord, whose confidence is in him. He will be like a tree planted by the water that sends out its roots by the stream. It does not fear when heat comes; its leaves are always green. It has no worries in a year of drought and never fails to bear fruit" (Jeremiah 17:7-8). You may be on the longer path for answers to your prayers because your root needs to grow deeper. Jesus explained His parable, "The one who received the seed that fell on rocky places is the man who hears the word and at once receives it with joy. (You asked Jesus to help you.) But since he has no root, he lasts only a short time. When trouble or persecution comes because of the word, he quickly falls away" (Matthew 13:20-21).

This is the same reason that the Lord knew the Israelites were not ready for battle even though they were fully armed. They were not truly rooted in their faith. One disappointment would have sent them back to living in the slavery that they came from. Again, I ask you, how deep are your roots? Do you lose faith in unanswered prayers and decide to turn back to your old ways? The Bible says, "So if the Son sets you free, you will be free indeed" (John 8:36). If you've placed your trust in Jesus, then you have been set free. But understand this: Just because you've been set free doesn't mean that your flesh (your inner desire) won't want to ever go back to Egypt. You've got to move away on your journey, far away from the temptation. The further you distance yourself, the more time that you've traveled away from your temptation. Hopefully, you are traveling and seeking the Lord's will for your life, and this will bring about deeper roots of faith.

Keep praying. God hears all prayers of believers. The answer may be yes, it may be no, or it may be not now. Many of our prayers are answered by "Not now." Take that as a sign that the Lord has chosen a longer path for you to get where He wants you to be. Work on developing deeper roots of faith. In this year of a slow economy, wouldn't it be nice to be like the tree planted by water in the scripture above from the Book of Jeremiah? "It has no worries in a year of drought and never fails to bear fruit."

I Don't Play Lotto

The title above may make you think that I am writing a lesson about the pitfalls of gambling. Even though gambling is a snare for many, this lesson is not about playing the lottery.

My daughter is enrolled in a statistics course this semester, and as I discussed this class with her I was reminded of when I took statistics in college. It was a hard class, but I actually did learn many useful things that I could really apply in the real world. (Not always the case in college.) I was explaining this in our conversation, trying to encourage her to take the class with a positive attitude. One of the comments that I made in our conversation was the fact that my statistics course ruined my desire to play the lottery. You see, when I am able to determine and understand the odds of winning, I just keep my money in my pocket. (I like good odds.)

Now don't get me wrong. My flesh (my body and mind) would love to win the mega-millions and retire to the beach. I get a little excited about buying a ticket when I read that Betty Sue won a million dollars in a scratch off at the local convenience store. But my intelligence kicks in when I start thinking about my odds of winning. I know that the odds are greater about me getting behind someone in line spending most of their weekly paycheck on several different lottery combinations when I just want to pay for my gas.

I was inspired to write this lesson by an e-mail that I received from a beloved friend this past week. My friend struggles with the concept of faith. My friend wrote, "I do spend a lot of time analyzing; I hope it isn't building up strikes with the man upstairs." In my response, I answered that I understand this position. I've been there, done that, bought a T-shirt. Not too many years ago I argued this same analyzing thing with my wife. I said, "There's no way that you can believe that Jonah was swallowed by a fish!" My wife answered, "Sure, I do." I didn't understand her answer then, but I do now.

The Bible says, "The fear of the Lord is the beginning of wisdom, and knowledge of the Holy One is understanding. For through me your days will be many, and years will be added to your life. If you are wise, your wisdom will reward you; if you are a mocker, you alone will suffer" (Proverbs 9:10-12 NIV). You see, all of my college and intellectual training just brought about more questions. The answers didn't start falling into place until I sought knowledge of the "Holy One"–Jesus.

Solomon wrote the Bible verse above. Solomon wrote the Books of Proverbs and Ecclesiastes. He was and is considered the wisest man who ever lived. Rulers of different lands would come from miles away just to spend some time with Solomon to gain wisdom. You can achieve this without traveling across any desert. Just pick up your Bible, and read through these two Books.

Solomon was also considered one the wealthiest men, even in today's standards. He owned many things and had many wives. Here is a man who seemed to have everything that one could ever want. He seemed to have all the answers, all the money, and all the things one could possibly need to be happy, right? We think sometimes that movie stars, music stars, and sports stars have all the things that could possibly make one happy. Then we read about divorce, drugs, or family and legal problems in their lives, and we see that they aren't so happy.

What is interesting to read about is the life of Solomon. Read through all of his Books of wisdom, read about his wealth, then read about his turning from God in the Book of 1 Kings. He receives his discipline for rebellion against God and in the end dies a sad man. The following Bible verse is written by Solomon as a conclusion to his life: "Here is my final conclusion: Fear God and obey his commands, for this is the duty of every person. God will judge us for everything we do, including every secret thing, whether good or bad" (Ecclesiastes 12:13-14 New Living Translation).

Perhaps as Solomon gained more wisdom he began to analyze things more, instead of trusting in the ways of the Lord through faith. Perhaps in his analytical reasoning he thought, "What's wrong with having many wives? I should be more politically friendly to their many different religions. What could possibly be wrong with me being a more accepting person? As long as they are being religious, worshiping their god, it makes sense not to be too close-minded." Well, being analytical, I can see his point. But it was not what God said.

You may say, "Well Robby, back to this fish thing. You said that you argued with your wife because it just didn't make sense to your mind. Surely you haven't fallen for that story now?" You know what? It's still hard for me to completely understand, but through my faith I believe it with all of my being. Jesus even referred to it in the gospel of Matthew, 12:40. You may say, "Well I just don't have that kind of faith." I say, sure you do. You just have your faith in the wrong kind of things: the ways of man.

I say that you have to have more faith in believing something like "The Big Bang Theory" (The theory that everything started by a cosmic big bang explosion that sent pieces of planets all over the universe), or the "Theory of Evolution" than I do in believing; if God said it, I believe it!

Let me give you an example by getting back to my statistics class:

What are the statistical odds of the following when this "big bang" happened?

Force of gravity: If the gravitational forces were altered by 0.00000000000000000000000000000000001 percent, neither the Earth nor our Sun would exist–you wouldn't be reading this.

Effect of the moon: The moon stabilizes the earth's tilt and is responsible for our seasons. If it weren't there our tilt could swing widely over a large range, making our winters a hundred degrees colder and our summers a hundred degrees hotter.

Earth's distance from the Sun: If the Earth were merely one percent closer to the Sun, the oceans would vaporize, preventing the existence of life. On the other hand, if our planet were just two percent further from the Sun, the oceans would freeze, and the rain that enables life would be nonexistent. (What are the odds that when the "big bang" happened that the above items lined up so perfectly?)

In your analyzing mind, does it make sense that we all came from the first living cell? One of our forefathers came to life by a chemical reaction out of nowhere? You have to analyze that nothing can come from nothing. I ask: from where did the "bang" come? Did you know that scientists have figured the odds of that first bolt of energy out of nowhere? For a moment, let's give the "big bang" the benefit of the doubt that it happened. Say the planet Earth landed here. Let's go even further and say by some chance there was a "warm soupy pool" of muck. Here are the odds of life forming that have been calculated by Donald Page of Princeton's Institute for Advanced Study: You have many times greater odds of buying all the parts for a TV set and going on top of a tall building and dropping all the parts at one time, and at the very first attempt a fully functional, HD ready, with stereo sound, television pops up.

Those odds calculated out to a chance in 1 out of 10124 followed by writing zeros all day long to the fourth power. It's just too big of a number to write. Here is a better statistical odd: Say you could get one grain of sand and actually make a mark on it. Then you were told to go anywhere in the world to randomly bury this single grain on any beach that you randomly chose anywhere on the Earth. Then you asked a random person to place on a blindfold and travel to any beach in the world, and choose one grain of sand. The statistical odds of that happening are one chance in 100 billion-billion, yet scientists tell us that the likelihood of life forming out of that first pool of warm muck are many times more improbable. I believe what God says, "In the beginning God created the heavens and the earth" (Genesis 1:1).

Let me share truth with you about being too analytical. The Bible says, "Since God in his wisdom saw to it that the world would never find him through human wisdom, he has used our foolish preaching to save all who believe" (1 Corinthians 1:21 New Living Translation). Hopefully my "foolish" teaching, sharing the Word of God with you, will draw you to learn more about Him and grow your faith. For, "faith comes from hearing the message, and the message is heard through the word of Christ" (Romans 10:17 NIV).

Today I encourage you to seek a closer relationship with the Lord. Give Him all of your analytical questions. I can share some wonderful statistical odds happening in your life for much greater value than the Mega-Billion Powerball can provide. (I put this to the test, and it proved out time and time again.) Draw nearer to the Lord and He will draw nearer to you. By the way—read my favorite Bible verse, (James 4:8).

Your True Value

On my way to the hardware store this week I pulled into the parking lot in front of the store. The store's sign said True Value Hardware. I thought to myself, "What does true value mean? Who, in the store, determines the true value of the product that I plan to purchase? Just because they say it is a 'true value' does that mean it is a 'true value' to me?"

Who determines your true value? How is your value determined? If you allow the "world we live in" to determine your true value, then what others think about you is the value that you place on yourself. If this is your value method, then your value, your self-esteem, will be like a wild roller-coaster ride with extreme highs followed by extreme lows. Does your value come from your own mind? Do you measure your value by the way you think that you look, by your personality, by the things that you may have or may not have accomplished in life?

Does your true value line up correctly with who God says you are? Our value should come from the fact that we are made in the image of God. Genesis 1:26 says, "Then God said, "Let us make man in our image, in our likeness …" God made you just like you are. He gave you the traits that you have. He wanted you to be different. The Book of Psalms139:13-14, the Bible says, "For you created my inmost being; you knit me together in my mother's womb. I praise you because I am fearfully and wonderfully made; your works are wonderful, I know that full well." You may think that you have flaws in your personal creation. Do you think that God's creation is flawed? Is that the world's value in your creation (what others think about you)? What value does God place in his creation (you)?

God thinks that you are a mighty warrior! Right now you may be thinking, "Robby, God may think I'm OK, but He wouldn't call me a mighty warrior." You say, "Actually, sometimes I feel kind of weak in the day-to-day living. You just don't know what I'm going through right now." I'm here to tell you today that God knows that you can accomplish much more than you can imagine. Have you been holding back on something because YOU didn't feel that you were qualified? I want to remind you today about where you should be drawing your strength. In Philippians 4:13, The Bible says, "I can do everything through him who gives me strength." Nothing is impossible with God's help.

Have you ever heard the saying, "When I am weak, He is strong?" Do you know where that saying comes from? Jesus tells us in 2 Corinthians 12:9: "My grace is sufficient for you, for my power is made perfect in weakness." God values you greatly. As a believer in Christ Jesus you have the gifts to be strong, successful, and a mighty warrior.

Let me now tell you where to find the term: "mighty warrior". In The Book of Judges 6:12 an Angel of The Lord came to visit Gideon. The Bible says, "When the angel of the Lord appeared to Gideon, he said, "The Lord is with you mighty warrior." Now, you may be thinking, "Well, you keep calling me a mighty warrior. Gideon was probably strong and fearless. How does this relate to me?" Let me tell you what The Bible tells us Gideon's response was to The Angel of The Lord. You see, Gideon was asked to get an army together to defeat the Midianites, who held the Israelites as captives. Gideon responded in Judges 6:15, "But Lord," Gideon asked, "how can I save Israel? My clan is the weakest in Manasseh, and I am the least in my family." Does this sound like a mighty warrior's answer? Does this sound like something that you might say if The Lord was opening a door for you to step through? Gideon's response was, "I can't do that. My family is poor, and I'm the weakest of the bunch." God had a bigger plan. God knows our strengths and weaknesses.

This is a great story. It applies today as much as it applied years ago. The Lord told Gideon in verse 16, "I will be with you..." Did you know that The Lord goes with you today? Through God's help, you can accomplish most anything that you really set your mind to. The Lord wants you to be successful in life. He values you greatly. "For I know the plans I have for you," declares the Lord, "plans to prosper you and not to harm you, plans to give you hope and a future. Then you will call upon me and come and pray to me, and I will listen to you" (Jeremiah 29:11-12).

I want to encourage you to read Judges, chapters 6 through 8 all about Gideon. Once Gideon gathered an army to attack the Midianites, God said to Gideon that he had too many men. This seems incredible because The Bible says that the Mideanites came with "their tents like swarms of locust. It was impossible to count the men and their camels; they invaded the land to ravage it" (Judges 6:5). God wanted Gideon and the Israelites to know that it was God with them who were going to defeat the Midianites. Gideon started with thirty-two thousand men. They sent twenty-two thousand away. This left them with ten thousand. "But the Lord said to Gideon, 'There are still too many men. Take them down to the water, and I will sift them for you." Always remember, what seems impossible to man (you), is possible with God: "for we walk by faith, not by sight" (2 Corinthians 5:7).

God reduced Gideon's army to just 300 men. You will have to read, as Paul Harvey says, "The rest of the story" on your own. God valued Gideon. God has great value for you. Your true value is in God's eyes. His valuation of you should be more important to you than what you think of yourself, and especially more than what others may think of you. If God holds you in high esteem, then low self-esteem is a false illusion.

To say God values us is to say God loves us. He does!

But God

I have been praying particularly and often for a dear loved one lately. I know that this person loves the Lord and has been calling out to the Lord for some answers and help in a trial that is taking place. I desire to offer words of encouragement, so I turned to the only Book that offers true hope and encouragement, the Bible. Perhaps this lesson may encourage you as well if you are currently in some sort of trial.

As I was reading through several encouraging passages, I noticed that many verses had the common words "but God" in the same sentence. This caused me to reflect back to the many trials that I have pulled through. Looking back I can see where the Lord was with me in each situation, but I also can remember that it was very difficult to sense His presence during that particular trial. I often felt that I was swallowed up by the trial that I was going through. In the Book of Acts, Luke refers back to the Old Testament story of Joseph. Joseph certainly went through many more trials than any of us will ever have to encounter, but Luke writes a very powerful sentence that should be an encouragement to you. In Acts 7:9 the Bible says, "But God was with him and rescued him from all his troubles" (NIV).

Now you may say, "Yes, Robby, that is a neat verse, but that was about Joseph and doesn't apply to me." I say wait just a minute; I'm here to tell you that God is with you and will deliver you from ALL your troubles if you are walking in His way. The Bible is God's letter (His Word) to us, and we are to apply the teachings to our daily walk. In the Book of Psalms, chapter 34 the Bible says, "I sought the Lord, and he answered me; he delivered me from all my fears" (v.4). And next, "This poor man called, and the Lord heard him; he saved him out of all his troubles" (v. 6). Did you get it yet? I'm not through; look at verse 17: "The righteous cry out, and the Lord hears them; he delivers them from all their troubles." I want to make sure you get this: Look at verse 19, "A righteous man may have many troubles, but the Lord delivers him from them all ..."

I would like for you to insert your name in the verse above and read it out loud so that you can hear it and take it in. Example: "Robby may have many troubles, but the Lord delivers him from them all." To help along with the title of my lesson you might read it this way: "(Your Name Here) may have many troubles, but God will deliver her/him from them all." Ok, go ahead, I'm listening, read it out loud using your name; I'll wait for you ...

I have so many "but God" stories in my own life. Many times I couldn't see how I could possibly overcome the task or trial that I was under. Actually, I couldn't, but God could. In the story of Joseph, Joseph was certainly in a trial because he had been in prison for a crime that he didn't commit. Pharaoh called Joseph to appear before him to interpret a dream. Talk about a task to achieve! How can Joseph possibly do this? Joseph gives us his answer in Genesis 41:16," 'I cannot do it,' Joseph replied to Pharaoh, 'but God will give Pharaoh the answer he desires.'" We often try to fix things, or even people, with many different remedies. One thing that I have learned through experience and my walk with the Lord is that I can't fix anything. Oh, I keep trying, but each time I finally just give it to the Lord after my failure. So I follow the passage in the Book of 2 Samuel 22:7, "But in my distress I cried out to the Lord; yes I called to my God for help. He heard me from his sanctuary, my cry reached his ears" (NLT). Notice that the passage has the words "but" and "God."

The loved one that I referred to in the beginning of this lesson is in a trial involving a health issue. I often wish that I had the answer to questions about failing health or why something is going wrong in a personal relationship. I can't give an answer as to why, but I can say give it to the Lord so you can personally see a "but God" story. The Bible gives a powerful testimony to follow in this situation: "My health may fail, and my spirit may grow weak, but God remains the strength of my heart; he is mine forever" (Psalms 73:26 NLT). But God remains the strength–His grace will be sufficient to see you through.

So many times in our lives, we experience a trial and get swallowed up in the difficult situation that we are in, and we can't see how any good can result out of the trial. In my years of experience, I can assure you that I have heard SO MANY testimonies of the good that resulted out of that difficult situation. Just wait for the Lord, and you too will have a "but God" story to tell. Just as Joseph told his brothers about being thrown into a pit and sold into slavery, you will witness the other side of the story. Joseph tells them many years later, "You intended to harm me, but God intended it for good to accomplish what is now being done ..." (Genesis 50:20 NIV). Your personal "but God story" may be a miraculous cure, or it may happen during recovery from major surgery, or even after a relationship break-up.

In previous lessons, I have shared how God reached down to me only after I called out to Him while I was in a trial. It is interesting to me to think back through all of the Bible stories about how God became involved only after the person humbled himself and cried out to the Lord. At the time just before my cry-out, I was walking in my own way. Often, I would sense God's calling to guide me in His ways, but I chose to ignore His directives, and I would just go in my own direction. Oh, I would sometimes think that I would appease Him by visiting church or by doing something kind, but I didn't want to give up going in my own direction with a few things in my life. Then one day I was swallowed up and went into deep distress ...

This morning, in my daily devotion time, I opened my Bible to get a little direction for my day. I planned to read some passages in the Book of Hebrews, but when opened, my Bible was in the Book of Jonah. I thought to myself, "I've read and heard this story enough. I don't need to spend any time here." I glanced down to the beginning of the Book and read, "The word of the Lord came down to Jonah ..." (Jonah 1:1 NIV). This caught my attention, and I thought, "Perhaps the word of the Lord will come down to Robby." It did! I didn't know that there was a "but God" line in the Book of Jonah.

The Bible says, "But Jonah ran away from the Lord and headed for Tarshish" (Jonah 1:3). Notice this verse says, "But Jonah" and not "But God." It's not a very good sign when things start off, "But Robby... or, "But (Your name here)." Very much like Jonah, I was going my own way. Are there areas in your life that you are headed in your own direction? In Jonah's journey of his own direction, he ran into a big storm (a big trial). It seems this happens more frequently (storms/trials) when we are on our own way toward Tarshish (away from God). Jonah paid a fare to enter a ship to sail for Tarshish to, "flee from the Lord" (vs. 3). The Bible says, "Then the Lord sent a great wind on the sea, and such a violent storm arose that the ship threatened to break up" (vs. 4). The storm was so bad that the ship was about to break apart, and all those aboard were close to being destroyed. Jonah realized that his disobedience to the Lord was affecting the lives of others around him. (Does your disobedience sometimes affect the relationships that are around you?)

Jonah became so distraught about the effect of his storm on others that he decided to give up his own life to give relief to the others around him. Do you sometimes think that the answer is giving up? That is NEVER God's desire for you! He only wants you to turn your ways to His ways. I'm certain that if Jonah went to the captain of the ship and said, "Turn this boat back toward Nineveh since I've decided to follow the Lord's will for my life," that the storm would have subsided. But Jonah chose to give up his life. He told the others on board to, "Pick me up and throw me into the sea" (vs. 12). They eventually did, and then, "the raging sea grew calm" (vs. 15).

You may think, "Robby, you just said that giving up is never God's will. It seems that once he gave up, all others around him were for the better." My answer is: God only wanted Jonah to follow the will of the Lord, not to give up. How do I know this, you ask? Keep reading. Instead of following God's way, Jonah AGAIN decides to fix something himself. Do you remember earlier that I said that I always try to fix something on my own, but only fail? Well, Jonah's way to fix the trial was to give up his life ... but God ...

The Bible says, "But the Lord (But God) provided a great fish to swallow Jonah, and Jonah was inside the fish three days and three nights" (vs. 17). God didn't want Jonah to give up his life; He wanted Jonah to follow His ways. So He provided a great fish that swallowed Jonah. I mentioned earlier that we sometimes get swallowed up in a trial, and we get deep in distress. What shall we do? When you feel swallowed up (overwhelmed) do as Jonah did, and as David did in the Psalm above, and as Robby did in his distress, and call out to the Lord.

The Bible says Jonah prayed, "From inside the fish (swallowed up in his trial) Jonah prayed to the Lord his God. He said: 'In my distress I called to the Lord, and he answered me. From the depths of the grave I called for help, and you listened to my cry … When my life was ebbing away, I remembered you, Lord, and my prayer rose to you, to your holy temple … But I, with a song of thanksgiving, will sacrifice to you. What I have vowed I will make good. Salvation comes from the Lord'" (Jonah 2:1-9). Jonah prayed, "Salvation (deliverance) comes from the Lord." Your best deliverance also has a "but God" in the verse, "But God demonstrates his own love for us in this: While we were still sinners, Christ died for us" (Romans 5:8). Jonah prayed that he was giving his will up and seeking the Lord's will with a vow to make good. I encourage you to do the same and vow to your deliverer (Christ Jesus) that you will seek His will and follow His ways.

After Jonah's submission to the Lord, the Lord commanded the fish to deliver Jonah up onto dry land. (That's the picture above.) Jonah submitted to God's will and the Lord's purpose for Jonah was fulfilled. You too are here for a purpose. Ask God to reveal His purpose for your deliverance from this trial. The Lord will save you and deliver you from ALL your troubles.

Getting Even

A special TV mini-series movie, "Master of the Game," aired in 1984 that was about prospectors going to Africa to find diamonds. Very much like the old gold prospectors going to California, the fictional made-for-TV movie had late18th century men going to South Africa to find diamonds. A deceitful man tricked the main character, Jim McGregor, very early in the movie. The once trusted man stole all of Jim's diamonds that he had worked so hard to find. The rest of the movie was all about Jim plotting revenge for the loss of his stolen goods. The famous line that I still remember to this day was when Jim found out that he had been tricked. He looked into the eyes of the man he had trusted and said with a thick Scottish accent, "You'll regret the day you met James McGregor." (Make sure that you roll your r's as you say the line like a Scottish person would.)

Through my years since watching this movie, I have often said this line to myself when I have been hurt or deceived by someone. At the moment of pain or hurt, I would say to myself, "You'll regret the day you met James McGregor." Then I would insert my name and think, "You'll regret the day you met Robby Stephens." (I wanted revenge and planned to make him pay!)

This lesson came to my mind this past week as I spoke with a young person who had recently been hurt by others. The impulse was to lash out verbally or to plan to "get even" in some way. I know that we all struggle with this idea from time to time no matter where we are in our walk with the Lord. Just the other day, I was driving on the interstate listening to praise music from my iPod. I came upon a slow car in the far right lane so I looked in my rear view mirror and saw that there was a car approaching in the next lane, but it was over 100 yards behind me. I kindly turned on my left turn blinker, which is not the "norm" in Atlanta traffic, and made the lane change with plenty of room. This young lady in the approaching car zoomed up to me and proceeded to blow her horn and flash her lights as if I had tried to run her off of the road. There were over three more lanes to her left, but she chose to pull up to my rear bumper and gave me the finger. My immediate reaction was, "You'll regret …" then I caught myself. I did as the prodigal son did in Luke 15: 17. The Bible says, "When he came to his senses …"

I love to read the promises of the Bible. I call them promises because they are from God's word to us. The Bible says, "Do not say, 'I'll pay you back for this wrong!' Wait for the Lord, and he will deliver you" (Proverbs 20: 22 NIV). You may be thinking, "What? Robby, what does it mean for me to wait for the Lord? You just don't know what this person did to me! There is no waiting. He needs to learn a lesson now!" I say I understand. I wanted to get behind that young lady blowing her horn and do a little NASCAR move of "bump drafting" and put her into the wall. But I didn't. I just remembered the Bible verse that I just mentioned, and I said it to myself.

We live in a world full of hurt and pain. Most times we just can't understand why some of the things happen to us that hurt us so badly. We have heard the promise from the Book of Romans: "And we know that in all things God works for the good of those who love him, who have been called according to his purpose" (Romans 8:28). But we often ask ourselves, "How can any good come from what just happened?"

I challenge you today to start asking the Lord this question when something happens to you that you just can't understand. I practice this suggestion each and every week. Then I just turn it over to Him. He tells us in Psalms 34:19, "A righteous man may have many troubles, but the Lord delivers him from them all …" I just wait for Him to deliver me from ALL my troubles. I have many real stories to share with you as I write new lessons, where I see the hand of God working deliverance in my life. At first I think, "Boy that sure seems like a coincidence. Could God possibly really take an active role in my life?" As the "coincidences" seemed to line up one after the other, I know that they are not only a coincidence, but are in His divine hand.

In the movie that I referred to earlier, James McGregor schemed for the rest of the movie to get even with the man who hurt him. I actually enjoyed seeing him plot to get even. That's what TV and Hollywood teaches us. It is no surprise that we seem to be able to react so negatively when we feel we've been wronged. But the Bible teaches about forgiveness. This is not something we enjoy doing when we are hurt. It is very hard to do.

How many times have you said what is referred to as "The Lord's Prayer?" This is the prayer taught by Jesus in Matthew 6. Jesus teaches us to pray, "Forgive us our debts, as we also have forgiven our debtors ..." (Matthew 6:12). Have you said that prayer? Do you know what you are asking God to do? You are asking for Him to forgive you in the very same manner that you have forgiven the people who have harmed you. In that very same chapter, Jesus goes on to teach, "For if you forgive men when they sin against you, your heavenly father will also forgive you. But if you do not forgive men their sins, your father will not forgive your sins" (Matthew 6:14-15). As hard as it seems to do, you are much better to let that anger go than to try to get even. The Bible teaches that, "There are six things that the Lord hates ..." (Proverbs 6:16). One of the six says, "a heart that devises wicked schemes ..." (Proverbs 6:18). I would take caution if the Bible says not to do something that "displeases" the Lord, but I *really* try not to do something that the Lord hates.

Several years ago, a man who had lots of authority over me through his job position angered me. At the time, I felt that he used his given authority to hurt my position in my employment. When I approached him with my concern, he said some very hateful things to me. I thought to myself at that moment, "You'll regret the day you met Robby Stephens." I often plotted for the day of opportunity to get even with him. I didn't like anything about him.

A few years later, I was in position to get him back, but just a little. If I chose to get him back at that time, it would have harmed him just a little, but I would have been doing as my father taught me not to do, "cut off my nose to spite my face." In other words, I would be harming my situation a little just to get back even with him. I chose to do the right thing and to not get even, but I didn't forget or forgive.

Many years later (actually four different employers and three different cities later) I was attending a church service, and my Pastor was preaching on forgiveness. I remember that I was sitting on the very back row and Pastor said, "I bet right now every one of you can think of someone that you have never forgiven for a wrong that they caused to hurt you." Immediately this guy's name popped into my head. I had not seen nor thought about him for years. When the sermon actually started I thought to myself, "I don't need to hear this. I don't have any problems with forgiveness." Well, I guess that I did have some problems with forgiveness. Right there and then I asked the Lord to please forgive me, and I said in my deepest thoughts that I forgave this man wherever he was. I put it behind me there and then.

I'm telling you the truth here: I didn't know where this guy lived, (it had happened over twenty years ago), but within a month of my church forgiveness, the owner of the company that I worked for called me into his office. He said that he had received a call from a man that I might know. The guy whom I had just forgiven wanted a job within the company that I managed. When I first heard his name mentioned; my heart burned a little with anger. I then "came to my senses" and reminded myself that I had forgiven this man. The very same person who had so much authority over me several years ago was suddenly working under me. I treated him well and actually began to enjoy him as a friend. He didn't work out with our company, but I know that wasn't the reason why he came. (This was just the Lord's reminder to me that God is in control.) After about three months, all agreed that this position was not right for him, and he moved on.

This story reminded me of the story of Joseph in the Book of Genesis. The brothers of Joseph threw him into a well and then sold him as a slave to a passing caravan. Joseph ended up in prison and must have been thinking, "How can this turn into good, Lord?" Several years later, Joseph was promoted to be in charge of all of Egypt, and his brothers came unknowingly to Joseph asking for food, due to a deep famine. (His brothers did not recognize Joseph at first.) Joseph could have really paid them back for the hurtful thing that they did to him in his past. When they recognized him as the brother that they had so badly mistreated, they became fearful for what Joseph had the power to do in revenge. The Bible says, "his brothers were not able to answer him, because they were terrified at his presence" (Genesis 45:3). After their father, Jacob, died, the brothers got very concerned for their safety. They said, "What if Joseph holds a grudge against us and pays us back for all the wrongs we did to him?" (Genesis 50:15).

Today I want to encourage you to be like Joseph. The Bible says for us not to get even with the people who wrong us. We are to turn it over to the Lord and wait for His deliverance. Joseph had to wait for many years to see his deliverance finally come. I can now look back at the man I thought had harmed me and see the positive effect he had on me. It has all turned out for the good. I am 100% convinced that if that episode didn't happen in my life way back then, my career path would have taken a different road. I wouldn't be living where I am today and working in the ministry. You wouldn't be reading this lesson right now, and you wouldn't be feeling the need to forgive the person that God has placed on your heart right this very minute …

Just ask God to forgive you for your unforgiveness, and in your deepest thoughts forgive the person or persons who have harmed you. You too will be able to one day say the same thing that Joseph told his brothers about their attempt to harm to him:

> "You intended to harm me, but God intended it for good to accomplish what is now being done, the saving of many lives" (Genesis 50:20).

If I Need You, I'll Call You

For most of my years of employment, I have worked in the sales profession. There are many great benefits that a job in outside sales offers, like the freedom of not going to an office each day, and the opportunity to meet many different people in the course of a year. But to be successful in sales you have to have a strong value of self-worth. You see, most people don't think that they need to see you or hear about the product or service that you offer.

I train new salesmen, and one of the early lessons that I teach is the fact that most of the time when you first approach a new prospect, understand that they will naturally say, "I'm happy with the way things are right now." This is just a natural barrier that goes up as they evaluate what you say, and the way that you present yourself. The fact of the matter is they may need what you have to offer in a very strong way. I suppose in this way of thinking, salesmen and God have something in common. We both will hear the common answer to our offer of, "If I need you, I'll call you."

Did you know that the Bible has a story that follows along these same lines? In the Book of Acts, chapter 24 the Apostle Paul was a prisoner and was sent to Caesarea to be tried by the governor Marcus Antonius Felix. Paul shared the message of Christ with every prospect to receive the offering of an eternal life with God. Paul felt that everyone with whom he came in contact was a prospect to receive the truth. In his letter to Timothy he writes, "God our Savior, who wants all men to be saved and to come to a knowledge of the truth"

(1 Timothy 2:4 NIV). So even when Paul was called before a judge such as Felix, he shared the gospel's truth.

As Paul shared with Felix, Felix must have felt that what Paul was offering was needed in a strong way, but his natural man kicked in with the barrier response of, "I'm happy with the way things are right now." The Bible says, "Several days later Felix came with his wife Drusilla, who was a Jewess. He sent for Paul and listened to him as he spoke about faith in Christ Jesus. As Paul discoursed on righteousness, self-control and the judgment to come, Felix was afraid and said, 'That's enough for now! You may leave. When I find it convenient, I will send for you" (Acts 24:24-25). In other words, "If I need you, I'll call you." Why do you think that Felix became afraid when Paul spoke of being righteous and living under self-control? Felix was the governor, why would he be concerned with judgment?

The answer is that we all have the laws of God written on our hearts. I've yet to hear a good explanation from a non-believer of God as to why man naturally knows that it is morally wrong to do certain things. Oh, we do have many people that go against these moral values, such as stealing, but I know that man knows naturally inside that it is wrong. The Bible says:

> God will punish the Gentiles (that's us) when they sin, even though they never had God's written law." (Before we had the Bible and knew the 10 Commandments.) "And he will punish the Jews when they sin, for they do have the law. For it is not merely knowing the law that brings God's approval. Those who obey the law will be declared right in God's sight. Even when the Gentiles, who do not have God's written law, instinctively follow what the law says, they show that in their hearts they know right from wrong. They demonstrate that God's law is written within them, for their own consciences either accuse them or tell them they are doing what is right
> (Romans 2:12-15 NLT).

Felix was afraid because his inner soul was telling him that he was hearing the truth. He just wasn't ready yet to receive what was being offered. The pride in him thought, "I'm happy with the way things are right now. I'll wait until this fear passes away by just sending Paul away."

Do you ever tell God, "If I need you, I'll call you?" You might even say, "Oh I know that I need You, but just not right now. Maybe when I finish school, or maybe when I get married, or maybe when we have a baby, or maybe when I get out of this job that takes all of my time, I will call for You again." Perhaps we all get this way at times. It probably goes back to our natural desire to be in control of things ourselves. In our society of fast food and microwave living, we like getting things instantly, but only when we need them. It's a proven fact that most household burglar alarms are sold after a theft has taken place. The thief has already come to steal. I'm certain that all people affected have thought, "I wish I would have secured that hedge of protection when I first thought about it before the theft happened." Jesus tells us that we have a thief that is out to get us: "The thief comes only to steal and kill and destroy; I have come that they may have life, and have it to the full" (John 10:10 NIV). Perhaps we should be seeking our Hedge of protection before we need one. Read my lesson with the title "Hedge of Protection" if you're not sure to what I am referring.

Felix may have thought, "I'm a good governor, I do good things for the people. I'll even do well by sparing the life of Paul. If there is a god, surely he will be pleased by my good works and let me into his heaven." I actually fell for this lie of the enemy several years ago. I too thought that by me being a "good person" and doing "good works" that I was assured a spot in heaven. Just like Felix may have thought that he's doing a good work for God in sparing Paul's life, I thought the same, by doing "works of good" in the church I was attending years ago. But God is much more interested in our obedience to Him than the works that we do in His name.

You may think, "Now wait a minute Robby. That's a pretty bold statement. Where can you find that in the Bible?" I'm glad that you asked. Actually, you can find it in several places, but I will cover only two in this lesson. First, turn to 1 Samuel, chapter 15. The first King of Israel, Saul, lost his rule as king because of his disobedience to the Lord's command. He did almost everything the Lord asked him to do, (a lot of good works), but he didn't obey all that was commanded. The prophet Samuel replies to Saul: "Does the Lord delight in burnt offerings and sacrifices as much as in obeying the voice of the Lord? To obey is better than sacrifice ..." (1 Samuel 15:22 NIV). David was anointed as king shortly after this disobedience.

The second example and passage is a pretty stiff penalty, but it clearly shows that God desires for us to be obedient more than doing good works for Him. King David wanted to honor God by bringing the ark of God back to Jerusalem. God had given specific instructions, originally to Moses, on how He wanted the ark to be carried. (Remember Indiana Jones and the Raiders of the Lost Ark?) The ark was to be carried on poles. Well they decided to do God some good works and bring the ark to Jerusalem—in a cart. (It was even a NEW cart according to the Bible: "They set the ark of God on a new cart and brought it from the house of Abinad, which was on the hill.") But this was not in obedience to the Lord's commands. Poor old, "Uzzah reached out his hand to help steady the ark, because the oxen stumbled. The Lord's anger burned against Uzzah, and he struck him down because he had put his hand on the ark. So he died before God" (2 Samuel 6:3-7).

Today I want to encourage you to renew your obedience to the Lord. Jesus says, "If you love me, you will obey what I command" (John 14:15 NIV). Don't fall for the snare of thinking that you will start being more obedient later. Later may never come: "Now listen, you who say, 'Today or tomorrow we will go to this or that city, spend a year there, carry on business and make money.' Why, you do not even know what will happen tomorrow. What is your life? You are a mist that appears for a little while and then vanishes" (James 4:13-14). James is telling us that our life here is very short compared to our eternal life, and tomorrow may never come. You may be thinking, "Now Robby, this obedience thing is hard. There are so many do's and don'ts to follow. How can I possibly remember them all?" My answer is, can you remember just one? Then remember this one, "Love the Lord your God with all your heart and with all your soul and with all your mind and with all your strength" (Mark 12:30). If you practice this, all the others will just fall into place.

Use a Nail as an Anchor

Just yesterday I spent some good quality time with my son Josh. We were working on a project together in order to prepare an old boat trailer to become road ready. Josh has a small boat that he plans to use the trailer to transport his boat to the fishing pond and back.

Our project yesterday was still on my mind this morning and it helped to inspire my new lesson. Often times our lives are described as boats out on the lake of life. We all desire to have calm water days like in the picture above. We would just as soon leave out the rough water days that storms (trials) bring into our life.

Storms blow in sometimes and really make our boat rock in violent ways. I don't like storms; whether it is a stormy trial in my life, or a violent storm outside like a strong thunderstorm. I want my life to be like that boat picture above, calm water and next to a dock for secure keeping, but storms will come. Jesus tells us in John 16:33 that, "In this world you will have trouble."

Writing about storms reminds me of a story from my younger life. I believe this memory is the reason for my fear of storms today. I was around ten years old and we were at my grand parent's lake house in Texas. As you know, everything is bigger in Texas and this goes for the lakes and the storms. I was fishing with my family on a pontoon boat way out in the middle of a large Texas lake. Some thunderclouds started gathering over the horizon and my grandmother cautioned that we should start heading toward the safety of our dock. I believe that we delayed leaving for a few minutes because we had found a good fishing spot. The clouds grew darker at the distant corner of the lake so we headed in. (This actually makes my heart beat faster remembering this part of the story.)

Suddenly the wind picked up and was blowing against us and causing the waves to make small whitecaps. Our boat was tossed up and down and our motor was not strong enough to move us forward against the wind at a very fast speed. The only thing comforting for me at that time was looking at my fathers face. As he drove the boat looking forward, his face showed the calm confidence that we were going to make it back safely. I had faith in my father to get me through the storm.

Just as we finally made it to our dock, my father reached out and grabbed the post connected to the dock. Boy, that's when the winds really hit hard. I can remember my father holding on to the dock as strong as he could as the ones that he loved climbed out of the boat to safety. Looking back on that, I understand the love that my Father in heaven has for both you and I. When in a storm, just have faith in Him that He will guide you back to the safety of the dock.

You may feel that your boat has drifted away from the security of a dock and you're in a storm right now. You may be under some type of trial where you feel that a furious squall has blown in and the waves are breaking over your sides to where you feel that your boat may be swamped under. You may be ready to cry out to the Lord, "Lord, don't you care if I drown?" If this is true, now or later, I say have faith! Place your trust in Him to get you through the storm back to the dock. Just one short Word from our Heavenly Father can calm your stormy lake.

In the Book of Mark chapter 4 there is a story about our Lord traveling in a boat across a lake with his disciples. As they approached the middle of the lake the Bible says, "A furious squall came up, and the waves broke over the boat, so that it was nearly swamped. Jesus was in the stern, sleeping on a cushion. The disciples woke him and said to him, 'Teacher, don't you care if we drown?' He got up, rebuked the wind and said to the waves, 'Quiet! Be still!' Then the wind died down and it was completely calm. He said to his disciples, 'Why are you so afraid? Do you still have no faith?'" Mark 4:37-40 (NIV)

Just as I looked to the face of my earthly father, Dad, when I was in a storm seeking some assurance that I would make it through the storm, you can look into the face of your Heavenly Father for your assurance to make it through your storm to the safety of the dock. You do this through your eyes of faith by prayer to Him. The Bible says, "A righteous man may have many troubles, but the Lord delivers him from them all." (Psalms 34:19)

You may think, "Robby, that is A Good Word, but what does the title, Use *A Nail As An Anchor*, of the lesson have to do with all of this boats and storms talk? I'm glad that you asked. Did you notice in the Bible verse above that the Lord says will be delivered from ALL of his troubles? Don't you desire to be delivered out of all of your storms of life? How do you become a righteous person so that you may be delivered out of all your troubles?

You stay in the Word and fellowship of the Lord. Many times in our boats of life we often aren't anchored to the dock... (A personal relationship with Jesus Christ). After a while we just tend to drift away from the safety of the dock. Did you know that in the picture above, if the boat were not anchored to the dock, even on a calm day, it would just drift away on its own? In our boat of life, if we don't anchor to the dock we may just drift out to the middle of the lake and suddenly find ourselves in a "furious squall."

I would like to encourage you today not to just drift around in your boat not anchored to anything. Anchor your boat to the safety of the Word of God. Did you know that you could anchor a boat to a dock by using a nail? If you tie your boat with a rope and by nailing the other end of the rope to the dock, your boat will not drift away. Even if you drift a long way from the dock, you can return no matter what your boat has been through. Come back to the dock and use a nail as an anchor.

The Bible says, "When you were dead in your sins and in the uncircumcision of your sinful nature, God made you alive. He forgave us all our sins, having canceled the written code, with all its regulations, that was against us and that stood opposed to us; he took it away, nailing it to the cross" (Colossians 2:13-14 NIV). Use the same nails to secure your boat to the dock.

Objects In Mirror Are Closer
Than They Appear

This lesson has a special dedication to you if you are going through a tough time right now. You are my "beloved reader."

My job demands many hours each week in my car. My car is basically my office. I actually enjoy my time driving because it gives me the opportunity to listen to my favorite music, my favorite sermons on tape, and other spiritual encouragement recordings. Many of you know that I am working toward completion of a master's degree from seminary. I often feel that my "class time" in my car has earned me enough credit hours to earn a doctorate degree.

As I was driving the other day, I felt burdened by the trial that you are going through right now. I was seeking A Good Word to pass along to you, a Word of encouragement. At a stop light, I glanced into the passenger side mirror and read the words written on the mirror. It said, "Objects In Mirror Are Closer Than They Appear." I started to think ... when you go through a tough time in your life, God seems like a very distant object. If you were trying to find His presence right now in your life, He may seem so far off it would be like looking for Him in that funny rear view mirror on your car. But I'm here to tell you today– like the mirror says –God is closer than He appears.

In your times of trouble, the enemy (Satan and his demons) is trying to make you look into that funny little mirror on your car to find God's presence. Your spiritual eyes become distorted, and you can't see the things that at one time you did see. When this happens, the thing you can't do is believe the enemy's lies. If you do, you will feel trapped and worried that there is no way out of your situation. What you must do is turn to a friend who is walking with the Lord. This person has a much clearer vision of God's presence in your life. Let me tell you about one of my favorite Bible stories concerning this type of trial.

In the Book of 2 Kings 6:8, the Bible says, "Now the king of Aram was at war with Israel. After conferring with his officers, he said, 'I will set up my camp in such and such a place'" (NIV). You see, the king of Aram wanted to capture and kill the army of Israel. He went around and kept setting up different camps in hiding. He was trying to trap the army of Israel. But the king of Israel had a man walking with the Lord, the prophet Elisha. Elisha would warn the king of Israel about where the army of Aram was located, thus the army of Israel would avoid the trap. This enraged the king of Aram, because he kept setting traps, but Israel would always avoid them. In 2 Kings 6:11-14 the Bible says:

> This enraged the king of Aram. He summoned his officers and demanded of them, 'Will you not tell me which of us is on the side of the king of Israel?' 'None of us, my lord the king,' said one of his officers, 'but Elisha, the prophet who is in Israel, tells the king of Israel the very words you speak in your bedroom.'
>
> 'Go, find out where he is,' the king ordered, 'so I can send men and capture him.' The report came back: 'He is in Dothan.' Then he sent horses and chariots and a strong force there. They went by night and surrounded the city (NIV).

Now this is where the story gets good! The king of Aram now set a trap not to capture the army of Israel, but a trap just to catch Elisha. At night, the army of Aram surrounded the city where Elisha was located, Dothan. (I believe it was Dothan, Alabama … not really.) The next morning the servant of Elisha got up early and walked outside. He saw a terrible thing. The army of Aram had surrounded the whole city with horses, chariots, and fighting soldiers.

The Bible says in 2 Kings 6:5 that the servant cried out, "Oh, my lord, what shall we do?" Do you think that this servant was afraid? Do you think that this servant felt like he was in a terrible trial? Did it seem to him that there was no way out? Do you think that God seemed like a small distant object in a funny mirror to this servant at this trial in his life?

In your trial, do you feel that you are surrounded and there is no way out? Does it seem that God is nowhere close by? Does it seem that you are looking to God to help you, but you just can't see Him in that funny rear view mirror where objects look so far away? Well, when you feel this way, I have A Good Word for you. God is with you! You may not be able to see his hand on you, but I can tell you, I see Him right beside you.

In the Book of Deuteronomy 31:8 the Bible says, "The Lord himself goes before you and will be with you; he will never leave you nor forsake you. Do not be afraid; do not be discouraged." The Lord is with you to fight your battles.

Now back to the story about Elisha. This servant is really scared. He runs to Elisha after seeing the surrounding army and cries out, "Oh, my lord, what shall we do?" Do you know what Elisha says? Look at 2 Kings 6:16. The Bible says," 'Don't be afraid,' the prophet answered. 'Those who are with us are more than those who are with them.'" Wow! What does he mean here? Here we have a man walking with the Lord that can see things differently than his servant that seems to be in a trial. Is this verse familiar to you in any way? Turn to 1 John 4:4. The Bible says, "You, dear children, are from God and have overcome them, because the one who is in you is greater than the one who is in the world." With Jesus living in your heart, God is greater than any of your enemies, any of your trials, any of your battles.

What could Elisha see as he walked with the Lord that the servant couldn't see because of his trial? In 2 Kings 6:17 Elisha prayed for his servant, "O Lord, open his eyes so he may see." At that moment, the servant could see what Elisha could see. The servant saw that God was with them in the trial all along. The Bible says in 2 Kings 6:17, "Then the Lord opened the servant's eyes, and he looked and saw the hills full of horses and chariots of fire all around Elisha." The hills were full of God's army. Angels of fire had surrounded the army of Aram and were ready to destroy them.

You may not be able to see God right now in your trial. Let me tell you though, you're looking through that funny rear view mirror. I can see that God is closer than you think. We just celebrated how close He really came. He lived among us. Ask Him to let you see His hand in this trial. He will show you that, "in all things God works for the good of those who love him ..." Romans 8:28 (NIV).

Under New Management

January comes each year, and often that means a new beginning. A sure sign of a desired new beginning is a business with a banner or sign out front that reads: Under New Management. We can often find these signs during the first month of the year, because we relate a new year to a new beginning.

What do these business signs typically mean to you when you see them posted out front? To me it reads, "The last manager in here was a total failure trying to run things. We've brought in new management to improve for the better." These signs will actually make me wary for a while. I will keep my eye out to see if the management has really changed.

Can this day be a beginning of a new time for you? Is it time for you to make a personal management change? How are you managing the day-to-day challenges that you face in this world? Do you seem to be going from one trial to another? If your life sometimes seems to be a daily struggle, then a bigger question for you is: Under what authority are you managing? You may ask, "What do you mean by 'authority'? I'm under no one's authority. I make my own decisions." If that is your answer, then sooner than later you will be posting a "help wanted" sign.

As a manager, (we all have personal management responsibilities) you operate under some sort of authority. It is through an authority you answer to from which you are given authority. In the business world, it is your boss who gives you the authority to make the decisions that you make. Likewise, the personal decisions that you make each day are under an authority higher than you. Your decisions are influenced from under the authority that you operate. Under whose authority are you making decisions?

The Bible says, "Jesus drew near and said to them, 'I have been given all authority in heaven and on earth" (Matthew 28:18 GNB). This verse tells me that there is an ultimate authority for each of us; however, we choose whether to be directed under His authority or the authority of another ... "So Jesus called them all together and said, 'You know that the rulers of the heathen have power over them, and the leaders have complete authority" (Matthew 20:25 GNB). The Apostle Paul explains the other authority this way: "At that time you followed the world's evil way; you obeyed the ruler of the spiritual powers in space, the spirit who now controls the people who disobey God" (Ephesians 2:2 GNB). I ask you again, under whose authority are you making decisions? Is it time for you to seek new management?

You may think, "Does it really matter under whose authority I operate? I'm just a guy/girl trying to get by each day." The answer is "Yes!" Do you have an internal sense of purpose in your life? There is a personal plan of hope and future designed especially for you! You just have to make sure that you are operating under the proper Authority to receive this management "perk." The Bible says, "I alone know the plans I have for you, plans to bring you prosperity and not disaster, plans to bring about the future you hope for" (Jeremiah 29:11 GNB). This verse may sound like the "management perk" that you might be seeking. It is often quoted to encourage us; however, the two verses following this Bible text are the real benefit of structuring your management to operate under the proper Authority: "Then you will call to me. You will come and pray to me, and I will answer you. You will seek me, and you will find me because you will seek me with all your heart" (Jeremiah 29:12-13). I don't know about you, but I like working under an Authority who will listen to me when I seek help and guidance. I choose to not miss out on any blessings that I may receive by following His directions.

One of the most famous women of the Bible is Deborah. You find her story in the Book of Judges. The Book of Judges is full of reminders about why Israel missed out on the blessings that were available to them. The Bible says, "After Ehud died, the people of Israel sinned against the LORD again" (Judges 4:1 GNB). In other words, the people of Israel again chose to operate under the wrong authority. It is interesting to read about this "mother in Israel" (Judges 5:7). Here we have a simple mother who chose to be managed under the proper Authority. She was used mightily to save the people of Israel from the distress of captivity of a Canaanite king. The Bible says, "Now Deborah, the wife of Lappidoth, was a prophet, and she was serving as a judge for the Israelites at that time. She would sit under a certain palm tree between Ramah and Bethel in the hill country of Ephraim, and the people of Israel would go there for her decisions" (Judges 4:4-5). The people came to Deborah for her judgments, but from where did she obtain her authority to judge?

We sometimes call the trials that we encounter in life "storms." Are you in any type of storm now? Did you know that by choosing to operate under the proper authority, a storm could be used as a good thing? How would you like for your "storm" to be turned into a blessing?

The story of Deborah is very interesting. The king of Canaan, Jabin, cruelly oppressed Deborah's people. It was through the king's army commander, Sisera, which power was given to these oppressors by the strength of nine hundred iron chariots. This military authority was just too strong for the people of Israel to oppose. But the Bible says the people, "cried out to the Lord for help" (Judges 4:3). Many times it takes a difficult trial ("a storm") in our life to prompt us to decide to make a management change of authority. Only the Lord can turn a storm into a blessing, but you must first submit to His authority. Do you know that you cannot receive authority until you submit to the authority over you? A business world boss would never give you authority to make a change unless you first submitted to his or her authority.

The Lord gave Deborah's authority to her because she submitted to do His will. Jesus received His authority from His Father through submission. He tells us, "To those who win the victory, who continue to the end to do what I want, I will give the same authority that I received from my Father" (Revelation 2:26 GNB). Deborah sent for the military leader of Israel, Barak, and commissioned him to go against the army and chariots of Sisera. Here we have the strongest military leader of Israel before a mother serving under proper authority. Do you know what

Barak's answer to Deborah was? The Bible says, "Then Barak replied, "I will go if you go with me, but if you don't go with me, I won't go either" (Judges 4:8 GNB.) Barak knew from where Deborah received her authority. She didn't have to tell him. When you choose to make a management change, under the proper Authority, folks around you will know. You can actually take down your banner that reads, "Under New Management." It will show.

Deborah went with Barak into battle. The Bible says, "When Barak attacked with his army, the Lord threw Sisera into confusion together with all his chariots and men. Sisera got down from his chariot and fled on foot" (Judges 4:15 GNB). Do you know what caused the "confusion" to Sisera and all of his chariots? A storm! I mentioned earlier that only the Lord could turn one of your storms into a blessing. The Bible says, "Lord, when you left the mountains of Seir, when you came out of the region of Edom, the earth shook, and rain fell from the sky. Yes, water poured down from the clouds" (Judges 5:4 GNB).

The Lord sent a rare flooding thunderstorm that totally mired all of the heavy iron chariots. The very things that the Canaanites thought gave them their authority (the iron chariots) were turned into useless handicaps. I ask you again, under what have you placed your authority? Could it possibly be in things or people in your life other than the Lord? The choice is yours.

I encourage you to make a change in management if you have placed your authority under anything or anyone other than the Lord. Deborah was a simple mother who chose to submit to the authority of the Lord. The Lord, in turn, gave her the authority to win the battle, even in a storm. You, too, can win the battles in the storms of your life.

Don't Go Back

We all have received some sort of guidance from a coach in our past. Perhaps at some point, you took some tennis lessons or golf lessons. You may have played a team sport in your youth, and you followed the instruction of the coaches for that team. If you participated in a choir, you were actually under the guidance of a choir director who coached the group to sing in harmony.

Coaches were a big part of my life as I grew up playing practically all of the team sports. To this day, I still look up to the people who coached me. As my children grew, I began to coach their team sports. I remembered what a powerful impact that my coaches had on me, so I made sure that I acted with the utmost integrity and respect for all. I see grown men today who call me Coach Stephens just because I coached them several years ago. This is a title of honor. (That's me in the picture above.)

The role of the coach is to instruct and guide you to be successful in whatever you are attempting. One of the all time greatest coaches was Tom Landry of the Dallas Cowboys. It seemed that he had his team in the playoffs year after year. In one particular interview, Coach Landry was asked what it was like to take a group of men and train them to be a team of champions. Coach Landry replied, "My job is to get men to do what they don't want to do in order to achieve what they have always wanted to achieve." I see my role as your spiritual encouragement coach. I desire to encourage you to do the things that your nature may not really want you to do in order to achieve the goals that God has for your life. I want you to be the champion that you are called to be.

In high school, one of the positions I played in football was defensive back. My job was to defend against the pass first; then I could look to stop a running play. I was coached not to be fooled by the enemy's (the opposing team's) deception of a fake run. But you know what? I didn't always follow the instructions of the coach. I would get so caught up in the game I would forget the training to do right. Sure enough, the enemy would act like they were handing the ball off to a running back, and I would come crashing in only to find the running back didn't have the ball. The quarterback would then have a wide-open receiver to throw the ball to, since I did not follow my instructions and forgot the lessons learned in training. I suffered the consequences and pain of not following my coaching by being deceived by the enemy.

We are all involved in a game called life. We, too, have an enemy that calls plays of deception just to get us away from being the champion that God calls us to be. As your coach, I encourage you to follow this instruction from this lesson: Don't go back!

I've read the following Bible verse many times. The other day when I read it, it spoke to me in a different way. I never thought about it the way that I will share it with you today. The Bible tells a new story about Jesus healing a blind man at Bethsaida in the Book of Mark. The Bible says, "They came to Bethsaida, and some people brought a blind man and begged Jesus to touch him. He took the blind man by the hand and led him outside the village. When he had spit on the man's eyes and put his hands on him, Jesus asked, 'Do you see anything?'

He looked up and said, 'I see people; they look like trees walking around.' Once more Jesus put his hands on the man's eyes. Then his eyes were opened, his sight was restored, and he saw everything clearly. Jesus sent him home saying, 'Don't go into the village'" (Mark 8: 22-26 NIV).

It's great to read about the different ways that Jesus healed. This tells me that there's not only one way for Jesus to work a miracle in our lives. What was interesting to me about this particular story is the fact that Jesus took this man by the hand and led him away from where he was and what he was doing. You see, just in the previous Book of Matthew, Jesus heals two blind men by only touching them: "Jesus stopped and called them. 'What do you want me to do for you?' he asked. 'Lord,' they answered, 'we want our sight.' Jesus had compassion on them and touched their eyes. Immediately they received their sight and followed him" (Matthew 20: 32-34).

Another Bible story in the Book of Mark tells us that a woman who just reached out and touched the garment of Jesus was healed from a bleeding of twelve years. So why was the blind man not healed instantly in Bethsaida when Jesus touched him? Jesus not only touched him, but also took him by the hand and led him outside of the city. Also, what's up with this blind man not seeing clearly on the first touching? And why did Jesus lead him out and tell him not to go back?

Are you in need of a healing in your life? Is there something going on from which you would like to break free? You may say, "Well Robby, I'm not blind." I say being deceived by the enemy is being blind to the truth. Just like I got caught up in that football game and was fooled into going after a running back without the ball, you may get caught up in this game of life, and you are pursuing something as empty as a running back without the ball. Your empty-handed running back may be some form of drugs or alcohol, pornography, lust, greed, or status. All of these items are the temptations of this world, and the enemy will try to deceive us into thinking these things will make us "feel" better and happy.

Just as Jesus led the blind man outside of the city, you may need to be led away from the things that you are involved in to be healed completely. This may mean away from your current group of friends, your current relationship, your weekend night's routine, your free time on the computer, or the addictive products in your home. Being healed in your current situation may only give you blurry vision. You may think that you are healed completely since you can see things better than before, (your vision may be like the blind man that says now he sees men as if they were trees.) This blurry vision is much better than being blind, but it's not the champion vision that God intends for you to have. You may say, "I see good enough Robby. I'm OK with where I am." As your coach, I say don't accept well enough. Without clear vision, you'll never be able to see the vision of God's best plan for your life. I'd hate to have to play defensive back today without my contacts. I would never know who had the ball, and I would fall for every trick of the opposing team (the enemy).

Ask the Lord to heal you from your sickness, hurting heart, or painful situation. Take hold of His outstretched hand to lead you away from your current situation. Follow Him. He will restore your sight of the future that He has planned for you. But most importantly, after He leads you out (listen to your coach)—don't go back!

Maintaining A Healthy Hedge

After over three years of writing lessons of encouragement, I figured that I should expand my offerings a little and go into advice about gardening. I know that many of you are into keeping your yard looking attractive so the value of your real estate investment remains healthy. This lesson is about maintaining your hedge.

Attractive, healthy hedges do add value to your property, but they can also add another very important benefit. Look at the picture of the hedge above. What additional benefit might this hedge offer?

You may have attended a football game at the University of Georgia and seen the hedge surrounding the playing field. This hedge certainly adds beauty to the stadium, thus earning the "tween the hedges" name for playing inside Sanford Stadium, but the hedge provides a layer of protection for the players on the field and the field itself. You may be thinking now, "OK, Robby, I came here for a little spiritual encouragement. I can watch the Home & Garden Channel for better advice on horticulture." That's a true statement, but hang on for a minute for A Good Word. The Bible speaks about a protective hedge, and I want to encourage you to maintain a healthy one.

I can remember as a young boy, my father planted a long row of hedges on the edge of our property. One of my jobs in the household was to water those plants. I hated that job! There was nothing worse than to be a young boy full of energy, standing still for what seemed like HOURS, going from plant to plant with the watering hose. Even though I moved from that house many years ago, I have driven by it and looked specifically at that hedge row. The hedge is about ten feet tall now and provides a nice barrier for the side of the yard. If I had not watered and nurtured those plants, there would be a scraggly hedge with holes and open places throughout its line.

Jesus speaks about a protective hedge in the Book of Matthew 21:33 in one of His parables: "There was a certain landowner who planted a vineyard and set a hedge around it ..." (NKJV). This certain land-owner set a hedge around it for protection. You may ask, "Protection from what?" Protection from the enemy! Read my next lesson, "It's Time to Come Home." I write about your enemy wanting to shoot out your streetlight so that you go about in darkness. This same enemy desires for you not to maintain your hedge. Your enemy, Satan and his demons, are as real as the visiting team playing the Georgia Bulldogs. When the visitors defeat the Bulldogs in Athens, as Georgia Tech did in 2008, they normally damage the protective hedge by breaking off large pieces as a memento of their victory.

"Now Robby," you say, "There is a big difference in the reference Jesus made to a hedge and to what you are inferring. He is just speaking about a hedge around this certain man's property." Oh, really? Apparently, there is some value to this hedge that Jesus speaks of. Let's look at the Book of Isaiah. The prophet Isaiah is speaking on the Lord's behalf when he says, "And now, please let Me tell you what I will do to My vineyard: I will take away its hedge, and it shall be burned; And break down its wall, and it shall be trampled down ... For the vineyard of the Lord of hosts is the house of Israel ..." (Isaiah 5: 5-7 NKJV). In this passage, the Lord is speaking about removing His hedge of protection from the people of Israel. Why? Because they were not properly maintaining a healthy hedge! (They turned their ways away from the ways of the Lord.)

I ask you, how are you maintaining your hedge? Do you tend to it at all? If not properly cared for, the hedge will begin to die, and gaps and holes will begin to appear. This allows easier access from your enemy. If you truly desire not to maintain it at all, the Lord will allow you to choose this, and He will just take it completely away like He did in the passage of Isaiah above. Please don't choose this!

If your maintenance practices of having a healthy hedge have fallen short recently, and you have a gaping hole for the enemy to attack you, I pray that the Lord uses me as a gap filler for you and your family until you repair your hole. The Bible says, "And I sought for a man among them, that should make up the hedge, and stand in the gap before me for the land, that I should not destroy it …" (Ezekiel 22:30 KJV). My prayers are for you to be encouraged by this lesson and for you to repair your hedge.

Now for my hedge maintenance advice: Turn to the Book of James, chapter 4. I've given you my favorite verse in many of my past lessons. I will cover it again today because it is always appropriate, but I will add the verse just before it today. The Bible says, "Submit yourselves, then, to God. Resist the devil, and he will flee from you. Come near to God and he will come near to you" (James 4:7-8 NIV). Do the things of God by following His ways; resist the evil temptations that WILL come your way each day, and develop a much closer relationship with the Lord Jesus. This action is like a super fertilizer for your personal hedge of protection.

Did you know that you had a personal hedge of protection? The neat thing about it is that it can also provide protection for your family. I pray every day for the Lord to keep and help me maintain the hedge of protection that He has placed around my family and me. I KNOW that my prayers have been answered. I encourage you to fertilize your hedge and ask the Lord each day to give you the strength to maintain your hedge around you and your family.

You may say, "Robby this is a neat analogy, but is there really a personal hedge of protection provided by the Lord?" Absolutely! Turn to the Book of Job, which many believe to be the oldest Book of the Bible. The Bible says, "The Lord said to Satan, 'Where have you come from?' Satan answered the Lord, 'From roaming through the earth and going back and forth in it.'" (Job 1: 8). You see, we do have an enemy roaming around seeking to destroy us. The Apostle Peter tells this to us again in 1 Peter 5:8: "Your enemy the devil prowls around like a roaring lion looking for someone to devour." Peter has personal experience with Satan being after him because one day the Lord Jesus looked at Peter and said, "Simon, Simon! Indeed, Satan has asked for you, that he may sift you as wheat" (Luke 22: 31 NKJV).

So as the devil was roaming one day seeking to destroy someone, God asked Satan, "Have you considered my servant Job?" (Job 1:8 NIV). Satan replied that he couldn't attack Job or Job's family because, "Have you not put a hedge around him and his household and everything he has? (Job 1: 10). In other words, God had placed a protective hedge around Job, Job's family, and all of Job's possessions. The enemy couldn't penetrate the protective barrier that the hedge provided.

I encourage you to thank God for His protective hedge around you and your family. Ask Him to show you where the gaps are in your hedge so that you may mend it. Many of you know that my son, Josh, had a trial with melanoma, which is a skin cancer that can be fatal if undetected. The night that he received the medical report about the melanoma, he came over to our house very upset. Seeing him upset hurt me the worst. But I looked at him with all the faith that I have and said, "You're protected." He didn't really know what I meant, but several days later before we received the clean bill of health after surgery test, Josh e-mailed me. He said in a very short one line sentence, "Your reply of, 'You're protected,' did the most for me. :)"

I pray that you maintain a healthy protective hedge.

Is Jesus One of Your
Facebook Friends?

I must start this lesson with an explanation of what facebook is to many of my older than college-aged readers; however, I have recently seen a trend among many people my age getting their own facebook page. Several months ago I overheard my daughter giving my wife, Julie, a hard time for setting up a personal facebook page. My daughter was cool with me having a personal facebook page, since I am involved in youth ministry, but she couldn't understand why her mom would want one.

Facebook is an Internet-based system of communication between friends. It started out in the college community of students, and I believe one had to actually be a student registered in a college to have a Facebook page. It has now practically replaced the traditional e-mail for most young people today. I suppose the unsolicited "spam" in e-mail pushed the younger generation to seek a system of communication that only allowed participation among selected friends. (You have to give approval to allow a person to become one of your Facebook "friends.") I joined Facebook in order to stay connected with my younger readers of A Good Word Ministry. I realized that my college friends were no longer

reading my traditional e-mails. I do think as the "older" generation begins
to move more into Facebook, the younger crowd will seek a new system
of communication that keeps us older folks out. I actually saw a posting
recently on a college student's front page of his Facebook from his
father, reprimanding the student for not calling home for a few days.
(Not the place to post a message like this.)

You may be thinking now, "OK Robby, thanks for the history of
Facebook, but what does this have to do with the title of this lesson?
Good question. Many times during the week I receive a notice that "such
and so" has asked to become one of my Facebook friends. I then have
the option to approve, reject, or ignore the request. If I approve, then
that person is placed on the long list of friends on my facebook page, and
I in turn become one of the long list of friends on their Facebook page. I
am honored when asked to be included in each requester's list of friends,
but here is what is beginning to happen:

I accept the invitation to be a friend, and then I send a personal note
to my new "friend," and I receive nothing back. (No response.) It's like
he or she is saying, "Hey, I want to add you to my list because you are a
cool friend to have listed, but I don't really want to actually communicate
with you." What concerns me is that I see this same trend developing in
many young "Christians." They have a desire to add Jesus to their
"friend" list, but they really don't want a personal relationship with Him.
Is Jesus one of your Facebook friends?

There is a very popular song that I really like. It is called "A Friend of
God." In the chorus, and I do enjoy singing it out loud, you repeat the
phrase, "I am a friend of God," over and over again. It does make me
feel good to sing this song, but what makes me feel better is the fact that
I know biblically that I am also a *child* of God. (You can be friends with
your children.) I caution you to be very careful in just being OK with
being a friend of God. If your desire is to just have Jesus as one of your
long list of friends for others to see, but have no personal relationship
with Him, you may just get locked out of the House when it's time to
come Home.

Jesus gives us a parable in the Book of Luke, chapter 11, about just
being a friend. The Bible says:

Then he said to them, 'Suppose one of you has a friend, and he goes to him at midnight and says, "Friend, lend me three loaves of bread, because a friend of mine on a journey has come to me, and I have nothing to set before him." 'Then the one inside answers, "Don't bother me. The door is already locked, and my children are with me in bed. I can't get up and give you anything (Luke 11:5-7 NIV).

The parable of Jesus goes on to tell us that the man inside the house did finally get up, after the friend continually knocked on the door, which teaches us to be persistent in our petitions (prayers) to God. But I ask you, who was already in the house with the One who had the bread? His children! Where would you rather be, outside as a friend asking for bread, or inside with The Bread of Life (Jesus) as one of His children?

You may think at this point, "Well, Robby, the friend did get bread. What is the advantage of being a child?" I say if your relationship with Jesus is only like one of your Facebook friends, then you may later end up standing at the door knocking without getting any response or help. (He may stop coming to the door.)

Let's look at Luke 13:23. Someone asked Jesus if only a few were going to get into heaven. (Who was going to get into heaven?) The Bible says:

Someone asked him, 'Lord, are only a few people going to be saved?' Jesus said, 'Make every effort to enter through the narrow door, because many, I tell you, will try to enter and will not be able to. Once the owner of the house gets up and closes the door, (there is that man in the house again) you will stand outside knocking and pleading, 'Sir, open the door for us.' "But he will answer, 'I don't know you or where you come from.' "Then you will say, 'We ate and drank with you, and you taught in our streets.' (You use to give us bread when we knocked.) "But he will reply, 'I don't know you or where you come from. Away from me, all you evildoers!' "There will be weeping there, and gnashing of teeth, (a bad place to be) when you see Abraham, Isaac and Jacob and all the prophets in the kingdom of God, but you yourselves thrown out (Luke 13:23-28 NIV).

My comments are in parenthesis for emphasis.

Here is another advantage of being a child of God, instead of only having Jesus as a friend: Children receive inheritances! I'm sure that you may call me your friend, but I doubt that my name will be included in your will. The Bible says in Ephesians 4:11 that, "Furthermore, because of Christ, we have received an inheritance from God ..." (NLT). What is our inheritance? The Bible says:

> For his Holy Spirit speaks to us deep in our hearts and tells us that we are God's children. And since we are his children, we will share his treasures – for everything God gives to his Son, Christ, is ours, too. But if we are to share his glory, we must also share his suffering. Yet what we suffer now is nothing compared to the glory he will give us later. For all creation is waiting eagerly for that future day when God will reveal who his children really are (Romans 8:16-19 NLT).

By now I hope that you are thinking, "Robby, I would much rather be a child of God. Perhaps my relationship with Jesus has been as if He were only a facebook friend–there only when I needed Him. How do I know that I am "really" a child of God?" The Bible says that, "His unchanging plan has always been to adopt us into his own family by bringing us to himself through Jesus Christ. And this gave him great pleasure" (Ephesians 1:5 NLT).

He wants to adopt you as a child. So how do you become a child?

> Everyone who believes that Jesus is the Christ is a child of God. And everyone who loves the Father loves his children, too. We know we love God's children if we love God and obey his commandments. Loving God means keeping his commandments, and really, that isn't difficult. For every child of God defeats this evil world by trusting Christ to give the victory. And the ones who win this battle against the world are the ones who believe that Jesus is the Son of God (1 John 5:1-5 NLT).

I repeat for emphasis, loving God means keeping His commandments. The Bible says, "For all who are led by the Spirit of God are children of God" (Romans 8:14 NLT).

How is your communication with God? The Bible verse above said that it gives great pleasure to Him to adopt you into His family. Do more than just adding Him to your Facebook "friend list." Communicate with Him regularly; ask Him to be your "homepage" so that you will be part of the true family of believers. Also, more importantly, when you receive a message from Him, make sure that you answer back.

Turn the Page!

It seems lately that many of my dear friends are going through difficult times in their lives. I receive telephone calls, e-mails, and prayer requests about the trying situations that so many are encountering now. Even at the office, my boss will ask me for good news in view of the slowing economy. You, as well, may be in much worry over the economy. I do view the cup as half full instead of half empty, because I know Who is in charge.

I have recently made hospital visits to people whose hearts are hurting and who desire answers. I wish I had all the right words and all the right answers to their thoughts and questions. I will share an answer with you that has been placed upon my heart. If you find yourself in a difficult situation right now, I have A Good Word for you! Turn the page!

I must tell you that you are only on a new page in your life. Don't stop reading in your book of life here! There are MANY more pages that follow. I understand that it is very difficult to see beyond the chapter that you are in, but you must convince yourself that there are new pages and chapters that follow. If I were to use my Bible to show you where your life is situated today, I would turn to the Book of Ruth, chapter 1. The Bible says:

So the two women went on until they came to Bethlehem. When they arrived in Bethlehem, the whole town was stirred because of them, and the women exclaimed, "Can this be Naomi?" "Don't call me Naomi," she told them. "Call me Mara, because the Almighty has made my life very bitter. I went away full, but the Lord has brought me back empty. Why call me Naomi? The Lord has afflicted me; the Almighty has brought misfortune upon me." So Naomi returned from Moab accompanied by Ruth the Moabitess, her daughter-in-law, arriving in Bethlehem as the barley harvest was beginning (Ruth 1:19-22 NIV).

(Do you feel as if the Lord has brought misfortune upon you?)

Perhaps I would turn to the Book of Genesis, chapter 37, and say that this may be where your life seems to be today:

So when Joseph came to his brothers, they stripped him of his robe–the richly ornamented robe he was wearing–and they took him and threw him into the cistern. Now the cistern was empty; there was no water in it. As they sat down to eat their meal, they looked up and saw a caravan of Ishmaelites coming from Gilead. Their camels were loaded with spices, balm and myrrh, and they were on their way to take them down to Egypt. Judah said to his brothers, "What will we gain if we kill our brother and cover up his blood? Come, let's sell him to the Ishmaelites and not lay our hands on him; after all, he is our brother, our own flesh and blood." His brothers agreed. So when the Midianite merchants came by, his brothers pulled Joseph up out of the cistern and sold him for twenty shekels of silver to the Ishmaelites, who took him to Egypt (Genesis 37:21-28 NIV).

Do you feel as if you're in a deep well with no way out? Perhaps you found a way out of the well, but your life is headed in a direction you didn't want or plan.

I could open up the classic story of Job, and show you the page you may be living in that story:

> When Job's three friends, Eliphaz the Temanite, Bildad the Shuhite and Zophar the Naamathite, heard about all the troubles that had come upon him, they set out from their homes and met together by agreement to go and sympathize with him and comfort him. When they saw him from a distance, they could hardly recognize him; they began to weep aloud, and they tore their robes and sprinkled dust on their heads. Then they sat on the ground with him for seven days and seven nights. No one said a word to him, because they saw how great his suffering was (Job 2:11-13 NIV).

(I can see that you are suffering.)

There are many more places in the Bible that I could show you the place in the story where you may be currently situated. But I can assure you of this: I wouldn't leave you hanging here, on this page. Right now you may only see that you are trapped in a bad place, and there is no way out. I'm here to tell you that there is a way out! You may feel like the servant of Elisha right now, found in the Book of 2 Kings. The story goes that the King of Aram was at war with Israel. The prophet Elisha would keep the King of Israel informed of every move of the army of Aram. King Aram therefore set up to kill Elisha. He sent his entire army to surround this one man of God. Early one morning, the servant of Elisha awoke and went outside his tent: "When the servant of the man of God got up and went out early the next morning, an army with horses and chariots had surrounded the city. 'Oh, my lord, what shall we do?' the servant asked" (2 Kings 6:15). (Now the enemy wants you to feel completely defeated.) In one of the e-mails I received, the writer says that he just wants to give up. He writes, "I feel like I am fighting, but I want to give up in the middle of this battle." That is exactly what Elisha's servant felt like doing! Just raise his hands to the enemy and say, "I give up. You win." But turn the page! The story continues; don't ever stop in the story before it ends! Do you know what happens next?

The prophet Elisha says something that seems very strange. "Don't be afraid," the prophet answered. "Those who are with us are more than those who are with them" (2 Kings 6:16). Let me give you the New Testament equivalent translation: "because He who is in you is greater than he who is in the world" (1 John 4:4). Paul explains this meaning in more detail in 2 Corinthians 12:9: "But he said to me, 'My grace is sufficient for you, for my power is made perfect in weakness.' Therefore I will boast all the more gladly about my weaknesses, so that Christ's power may rest on me." In our moments of weakness and fear, we must turn it over to the Lord to handle. We can't win on our own strength. The Lord is there to fight our battles if we just submit them to Him. What do you think would have happened if Elisha's servant picked up a spear and ran towards the army of Aram to "fix" things on his own? What would have happened if he raised his hands and said, "I give up"? Both outcomes would have been tragic. But let me be like Elisha here to you: I pray that the Lord opens your eyes of faith! The Bible says, "And Elisha prayed, "O Lord, open his eyes so he may see" (2 Kings 6:17). You may ask, "Robby, what am I suppose to see, and what did the servant see?" I pray that the "eyes of your heart" are open that you would see that the Lord is with you to give you the strength to turn the page … and keep going. The Bible says, "Then the Lord opened the servant's eyes, and he looked and saw the hills full of horses and chariots of fire all around Elisha" (2 Kings 6:17). The Lord had His army of angels poised and ready to defeat the army of Aram.

I encourage you to lay your trial at the feet of our Lord Jesus. The Bible says, "Cast all your anxiety on him because he cares for you" (1 Peter 5:7 NIV). I understand that this is difficult to do. We act like we want to "cast" our anxieties on Him, but inside we still hold on to them thinking that we need to do something to "fix" them. This reminds me of my dog, Gauge, a black Labrador Retriever. By instinct he should retrieve, and he does. My son, Josh, trained to him to fetch, bring the object, and put it down at the feet of his master. (Kind of like laying your trial at the feet of our Lord.) But over time, without the act of continued discipline, Gauge now makes me wrestle it out of his mouth. He wants me to have it, but I have to wrestle to get it. Over time, you may have moved from the discipline of casting all your anxiety on Him. Don't wrestle your trials from the Lord. Just drop them down at His feet.

In your own story, you are just on one page of many to come. In the Bible stories above, we get to read about the final outcomes. We see and learn by the examples, that by allowing our Lord to do His will in our trials, the ending is much different than what it seems at the time. At the end of the story of Ruth, Ruth gets married to a wealthy man of God and has his child. The child is named Obed, who became the grandfather of King David. Her family tree is traced down to Christ Jesus Himself. At the end of the story of Joseph, Joseph becomes second in charge in the land of Egypt. He eventually saves his brothers, who threw him into a dry well, from starvation. The tribes of Israel are saved in the end by the favor of the Lord upon Joseph. At the end of the story of Job, the Bible says:

> The Lord blessed the latter part of Job's life more than the first. He had fourteen thousand sheep, six thousand camels, a thousand yoke of oxen and a thousand donkeys. And he also had seven sons and three daughters. The first daughter he named Jemimah, the second Keziah and the third Keren-Happuch. Nowhere in all the land were there found women as beautiful as Job's daughters, and their father granted them an inheritance along with their brothers (Job 42:12-15).

(The Bible says that Job was twice as blessed at the end of the story.)

Just like the Bible stories above, your story has an ending. You're just not there yet. Don't stop to think the place you are in now is the end. Jesus tells us, "Therefore I tell you, do not worry about your life … But seek first his kingdom and his righteousness, and all these things will be given to you as well" (Matthew 6:25-33). Seek the Lord and His will for your life, and He will provide the things that you need. This page in your life will pass. Recognize that you are in the middle chapter, even though things seem very difficult now. Trust in the Lord to deliver you: "The righteous cry out, and the Lord hears them; he delivers them from all their troubles" (Psalms 34:17). Remember, when you are in a difficult moment in your life, say to the Lord, "Thank You Lord for carrying this burden for me. I recognize that this is not the end of the story. Thank You for allowing me to turn the page."

It's Time to Come Home

C an you read the title and look at the picture above, and relate the two? You may have to think about it for a moment, but if you're near my age, you may know exactly how they relate. I will have to explain it to my wife and others like her, because she grew up outside the city where there were no streetlights on her street.

I had the good fortune of growing up in a neighborhood full of houses and full of children to play with. Even though I enjoy playing with a Playstation video game now, I believe that we were blessed not to have games like that to keep us indoors. We actually had outdoor "sandlot" baseball games in open fields. The children of the neighborhood would all come together, and we would play for hours without the need for umpires and uniforms.

As the games played out, it would begin to get dark. The one thing that we all had in common was the moment when it was time to come home. We almost instinctively knew that when the streetlights came on that it was a sign for us to be on our way home. We would use the light from the streetlight to guide our walk safely home.

Is there a light in your life now asking you to come home? You may think, "Robby, I am home. I'm in my chair reading your book." I understand, but do you need a little light to shine to guide you through something that you may not see a way out of right now? Perhaps you are walking in the dark without even knowing it. Are you wandering around through something and need a little light to shine on the proper path to take you back to your direction of purpose in your life?

In the book of Genesis, chapter 37, there is the story of Joseph wandering around looking for his destiny. His father, Jacob, had asked Joseph to, "Please go and see if it is well with your brothers and well with the flocks, and bring back word to me" (Genesis 37:14 NKJV). God had a wonderful plan and destiny for Joseph, but Joseph needed a little direction as he set out on his path to his purpose. I pray that the Lord uses me as the next character mentioned in this story. We never hear his name, and he never receives attention for what he provides. The Bible says, "Now a certain man found him, and there he was, wandering in the field. And the man asked him, saying, 'What are you seeking?'" This "certain man" provided Joseph with just enough direction to get him back on his path of purpose.

I would like to ask you, "What are you seeking?" Perhaps your answer is, "I would love to find my purpose, but right now I just need a little light to shine in this trial that I'm in. I can't seem to find my way out." The neat thing about an automatic streetlight is that it cuts on just as you need it. A relationship with Jesus is like having an automatic streetlight; just as things get dark, a light begins to shine to guide you through. The Bible says, "You are my lamp, O Lord; the Lord turns my darkness into light" (2 Samuel 22:29 NIV).

If, however, things seem really dark now and you are just "wandering," maybe you need direction from me. Maybe some vandal trying to keep you in the darkness has shot out your automatic streetlight. (You have an enemy that desires to keep you in the dark.) If that is the case, let me loan you my flashlight. You may need it just long enough to find your lamp in your own house. It's there, and it has a bulb that will always give light. In Psalm 119:105 we find, "Your word is a lamp to my feet and a light for my path." Your lamp is your Bible.

You may ask, "Robby, I know that you are full of faith and believe in this Bible thing, but how will reading my Bible really help me now? It's just full of words and stories written by man, isn't it?" Well, it was written by man, but look at the next Bible verse. (I keep this verse on my web page in the upper left corner.) It comes from the Book of 2 Timothy 2:16-17, "All scripture is God-breathed and is useful for teaching, rebuking, correcting and training in righteousness, so that the man of God may be thoroughly equipped for every good work." God-breathed means that the Lord Himself inspired all of the writings. These ARE the Words of God speaking to you and me! The Bible also says, "because our gospel came to you not simply with words, but also with power, with the Holy Spirit and with deep conviction" (1 Thessalonians 1:5).

It is difficult to understand in our human thinking, but there is power in God's words. That's why I try to fill each lesson that I write full of scripture. If you ever feel moved, encouraged, or convicted by anything that I write, it's not me. It's the Scripture; it's God speaking to you!

Let's look a little more into the words "God-breathed." We first find them in Genesis 2:7, "the Lord God formed the man from dust of the ground and breathed into his nostrils the breath of life, and the man became a living being." Later, in the Book of John, after the resurrection of Jesus, Jesus speaks to His disciples and says, "Peace be with you! As the Father has sent me, I am sending you. And with that he breathed on them and said, 'Receive the Holy Spirit'" (John 20: 21-22). Therefore, with the Bible being God-breathed, when you read the Bible–the breath of God (the Holy Spirit) rises from the pages to fill your heart. The words have power, so when you need light to guide your path, turn on your lamp by opening your Bible. The Bible says, "The unfolding of your words gives light; it gives understanding to the simple" (Psalm 119:130).

Well, it's been fun spending time with you, but the streetlight has just turned on, and it's time for you to come home and follow the light to get there safely. Jesus says, "I am the light of the world. Whoever follows me will never walk in darkness, but will have the light of life" (John 8:12).

The End of the Book

I recently did something that I don't normally like to do. I purchased a new book and immediately turned to the end of the book and read the last chapters. I normally don't want to know how a book ends before I read how it all begins, but I actually purchased this book just to see how it ended. I pretty much knew the beginning of the story. The beginning was a big part of my early life.

One of the titles that I considered for this lesson was "Become Your Hero!" My childhood hero was Pistol Pete Maravich. I came to know about "The Pistol" when he was in college, and I was in junior high school. Pete Maravich played basketball for Louisiana State University and was setting all time college records for scoring. I still have a ribbon in a scrapbook that I won doing a junior high school math project demonstrating the average of Pistol Pete's scoring in his games. If you could see his full jersey number above, it would show number 44 in his rookie year with the pro team Atlanta Hawks. Pete averaged 44 points per game in his college career, a record that still stands!

I wanted to grow up and be like Pistol Pete. I was fortunate to be able to go to see Pete play several games for the Atlanta Hawks. I would watch him play and then go home and practice for hours the basketball moves that I saw him perform in the games. My skill level never came close to Pete's, but I did turn out to be a pretty good high school basketball player. The name "Pistol Robby" didn't really go together, but one day one of my good friends on my basketball team called out to me, "Shotgun Stephens." The name stuck, and even today when I see some of my old high school friends, they call me "Gun" for a short nickname. (Vaughan, I'm thinking about you right now.)

You may be thinking now, "Cute story, Robby, but what does this have to do with sharing your faith?" As always, I'm glad that you asked. Back to my book ...

The book that I purchased has the title *Maravich*. It is the first biography of Pete Maravich that was in collaboration with Pete's wife Jackie Maravich. This is important because she tells the story of the end of the book. The first chapter in the book is called "Birth Of A Legend" and pretty much starts out like any biography, telling the story of where the subject is born. But the last chapters are titled, "Reborn" and "Purpose Driven Life."

The chapter just before "Reborn" is called "Withdrawal," and it reminds me of the Book of Ecclesiastes written by King Solomon. Like King Solomon, Pete had accumulated a great deal of wealth. He purchased all of the things that he thought could buy happiness and fulfillment. Solomon writes about this:

> I denied myself nothing my eyes desired; I refused my heart no pleasure. My heart took delight in all my work, and this was the reward for all my labor. Yet when I surveyed all that my hands had done and what I toiled to achieve, everything was meaningless, a chasing after the wind; nothing was gained under the sun ... So I hated life, because the work that is done under the sun was grievous to me. All of it is meaningless, a chasing after the wind. I hated all the things I had toiled for under the sun... (Ecclesiastes 2: 10-11, 17-18 NIV).

Pete had everything that money could buy, but like Solomon, Pete hated life. A passage from the book *Maravich* reveals one of his lowest points. He began to think about suicide. One night, as he drove his Porsche along the 23-mile Ponchartrain Causeway, he had an ominous thought that he just might drive off the bridge to commit suicide. Has the enemy ever whispered these kinds of thoughts into your ear? If so, perhaps you were/are trying to fill that empty hole in your heart with things and pleasures. You could be "chasing the wind."

I watched a neat video this morning when I first turned on the TV. It was on the VH1 video channel, something that I don't normally look at first thing, but the TV was on this channel when I turned it on. The video is called "Saving Me" by a band called Nickelback, from their album *All the Right Reasons*. I'm not exactly sure, but I believe this rock band is sending out a Christian message in this song. The words of the song say,

> "All I need is you
> Come please I'm callin'
> **And oh I scream for you**
> Hurry, I'm fallin'
> Show me what it's like
> To be the last one standing
> And teach me wrong from right
> And I'll show you what I can be
> Say for me
> Say it to me
> And I'll leave this life behind me
> Say it if it's worth saving me."

The neat thing about the video is everyone's head is an electronic timer counting down the minutes and seconds of each person's life. Only a few people can see the timer, but those are the ones most concerned for the others around them. (Just like I'm concerned for you!) We, too, have a clock counting down our time here on earth. The Bible says, "There is a time for everything, and a reason for every activity under heaven: a time to be born and a time to die ..." (Ecclesiastes 3:1-2). Our timer has a pre-assigned timed out number that none of us knows here, but God has assigned it. Psalm 39 of David says, "Show me, O Lord, my life's end and the number of my days; let me know how fleeting is my life. You have made my days a mere handbreadth; the span of my years is as nothing before you. Each man's life is but a breath" (Psalm 39: 4-5).

Pistol Pete's timer timed out very early in his life. He was only 40 years old and left a wife and two young sons. Thank goodness, his life didn't end in chapter 23 with the chapter titled "Withdrawal." At that time in his life, he was searching for all of the wrong things to fill that void in his heart. He was asking the same type of questions that I'm asked from time to time: Why am I here? What is my purpose? I want to ask you, what chapter are you in when you look at your life? What would be the title of the last chapter if your life were to suddenly end today? How would the end of your book read?

The end of Pete's book is very similar to another lesson that I shared with you. I wrote about the movie character Judah Ben Hur, and how Ben Hur fell down and cried out to God when he was at his lowest point in life. He was just about ready to give up on life when he fell and cried out, "God, help me!" At that very moment, in the movie, the shadow of Jesus covered Ben Hur. Jesus was there! The Bible says, "In my distress I called to the Lord; I called out to my God. From his temple he heard my voice; my cry came to his ears" (2 Samuel 22:7).

The end of Pete's book reads that he remembered the many letters from fans praying for his salvation. Pete believed that the people who wrote the letters were weak and threw their letters in the trash. Then, as he wrote in his autobiography, he had a revelation: He could no longer ignore the sin that was in his life. He sank to his knees at the foot of the bed. With tears streaming down his face, he cried out for God to forgive him. He asked God if He would really forgive him.

Psalms 130:1-4 answers Pete's question: "Out of the depths I cry out to you, O Lord; O Lord, hear my voice. Let your ears be attentive to my cry for mercy. If you, O Lord, kept a record of sins, O Lord, who could stand? But with you there is forgiveness: therefore you are feared." The same Jesus that showed up for Ben Hur upon his cry showed up for Pete Maravich. The same Jesus showed up for me when I cried out and my life was changed. Jesus is in the life changing business!

I wrote earlier in this lesson that my title could have been, "Become Your Hero." I now feel that I've reached that aspiration. Not that I was ever all that great at basketball, but I'm now doing what Pete was doing when his end of the book took place. Pete ended his book, (his life) sharing his faith with as many people as he could. His last chapter is titled "Purpose Driven Life." Perhaps if my life were to end tomorrow, my wife could use that same title to write about me. Perhaps you would buy the book and immediately turn to the end of the book to see how it ends.

Did you know that Pistol Pete Maravich's life ended doing the two things that he loved the most? (Sharing his faith while playing basketball.) He had heart failure on January 5, 1988 while he was playing a "pick-up" basketball game with church friends. He died on the basketball court in the arms of Dr. James Dobson of Focus on the Family Ministries. Dr. Dobson had traveled to meet Pete for the very first time to interview Pete for his ministry show. What a way to end a book ...

How will your book end? I encourage you today to work toward a good ending for your book. "Whatever you do, work at it with all your heart, as working for the Lord, not for men, since you know that you will receive an inheritance from the Lord as a reward. It is the Lord Christ you are serving" (Colossians 3: 23-24). The middle chapter of your book can be titled "Purpose Driven Life" if you start to live more for Jesus today. Perhaps when others buy your book, they, too, will turn to the end. Hopefully the title will read, "A Friend of God" (James 2:23).

This is the end my first book. I have more chapters to write ...